GOVERNMENT PROCEDURES AND OPERATIONS

NONCOMPETITIVE FEDERAL CONTRACTING

ANALYSES OF "BRIDGE" SITUATIONS AND URGENT NEEDS

GOVERNMENT PROCEDURES AND OPERATIONS

Additional books in this series can be found on Nova's website under the Series tab.

Additional e-books in this series can be found on Nova's website under the eBooks tab.

GOVERNMENT PROCEDURES AND OPERATIONS

NONCOMPETITIVE FEDERAL CONTRACTING

ANALYSES OF "BRIDGE" SITUATIONS AND URGENT NEEDS

JANET WEAVER
EDITOR

NOVINKA
New York

Library of Congress Cataloging-in-Publication Data

ISBN: 978-1-63485-153-4

Published by Nova Science Publishers, Inc. † New York

CONTENTS

PREFACE

When an existing contract is set to expire but the follow-on contract is not ready to be awarded, the government can extend the existing contract or award a short-term sole-source contract to avoid a gap in service. These have been referred to as "bridge contracts." While bridge contracts can be necessary tools, they are awarded without competition, which puts the government at risk of paying too much. This book examines insights selected agencies have into their use of bridge contracts; key characteristics of bridge contracts; and the reasons bridge contracts are used.

In: Noncompetitive Federal Contracting
Editor: Janet Weaver
ISBN: 978-1-63485-153-4

Chapter 1

SOLE SOURCE CONTRACTING: DEFINING AND TRACKING BRIDGE CONTRACTS WOULD HELP AGENCIES MANAGE THEIR USE*

United States Government Accountability Office

ABBREVIATIONS

BOP	Federal Bureau of Prisons
CLIN	Contract Line Item Number
DEA	Drug Enforcement Administration
DLA	Defense Logistics Agency
DOD	Department of Defense
DOJ	Department of Justice
HCAA	Army Health Care Acquisition Activity
HHS	Department of Health and Human Services
HIS	Indian Health Service
J&A	Justification and Approval
FAR	Federal Acquisition Regulation

* This is an edited, reformatted and augmented version of The United States Government Accountability Office publication, GAO-16-15, dated October 2015.

FPDS-NG	Federal Procurement Data System-Next Generation
NIH	National Institutes of Health
OMB	Office of Management and Budget
OFPP	Office of Federal Procurement Policy

WHY GAO DID THIS STUDY

When an existing contract is set to expire but the follow-on contract is not ready to be awarded, the government can extend the existing contract or award a short-term sole-source contract to avoid a gap in service. These have been referred to as "bridge contracts." While bridge contracts can be necessary tools, they are awarded without competition, which puts the government at risk of paying too much. GAO was asked to review federal agencies' use of bridge contracts. This report examines (1) insights selected agencies have into their use of bridge contracts; (2) key characteristics of bridge contracts; and (3) the reasons bridge contracts are used.

Because bridge contracts are not defined in the FAR, GAO constructed a definition based on its prior work and that of other federal agencies. GAO reviewed policies and procedures at three agencies that were among those with the highest number of potential bridge contracts. GAO analyzed a nongeneralizable sample of 73 contracts for services, based on a customized search of the federal procurement data system and contract information provided by agencies. For a more in-depth review, GAO selected a subset of 29 contracts based on contract value and other factors.

WHAT GAO RECOMMENDS

GAO recommends that OFPP take steps to amend the FAR to incorporate a definition of bridge contracts, and, in the interim, provide guidance for agencies to track and manage their use. OFPP agreed with the recommendation to provide guidance to agencies and plans to explore the value of adding a definition to the FAR.

WHAT GAO FOUND

The agencies included in GAO's review—the Departments of Defense (DOD), Health and Human Services, and Justice—had limited or no insight into their use of bridge contracts, as bridge contracts were not defined or addressed in department-level guidance or in the Federal Acquisition Regulation (FAR). However, GAO found that two DOD components, the Navy and Defense Logistics Agency, have instituted definitions, policies, and procedures to manage and track their use. The components took these steps due to concerns that bridge contracts were being used too frequently and reducing competition. Federal internal control standards stipulate that management should identify, analyze, and monitor risks associated with achieving objectives, such as maximizing competition. Staff from the Office of Federal Procurement Policy (OFPP), which provides direction for government-wide procurement policies so as to promote efficiency and effectiveness in government acquisitions, acknowledge that the use of bridge contracts may introduce risks related to a lack of competition. Without a definition of bridge contracts and guidance for tracking and managing their use, agencies are not able to fully identify and monitor these risks and increase opportunities for competition.

The 73 bridge contracts GAO analyzed varied widely in characteristics such as the type of service and length of contract. Almost half of the contracts were used to procure either professional management services or information technology services. Although bridge contracts are typically envisioned as short-term, GAO found that some bridge contracts spanned multiple years, potentially undetected by approving officials. For example, of the 29 contracts GAO reviewed in-depth, 6 were longer than 3 years.

Even after lengthy bridge contract scenarios, most follow-on contracts were awarded competitively. Of the 26 cases in GAO's review where follow-on contracts were awarded, 23 were awarded competitively, in some instances leading to savings. The fact that competition occurred in almost all cases, which can save the government money, highlights the importance of better management controls over use of bridge contracts.

Acquisition planning delays, such as revisions to statements of work and delays in source selection, as well as an inexperienced and overwhelmed acquisition workforce, bid protests, and budget uncertainties contributed to the use of bridge contracts in the cases GAO studied. Often, more than one of these factors led to the use of a bridge contract.

October 14, 2015

The Honorable Ron Johnson
Chairman

The Honorable Thomas R. Carper
Ranking Member
Committee on Homeland Security and Governmental Affairs
United States Senate

The Honorable Claire McCaskill
Ranking Member
Permanent Subcommittee on Investigations
Committee on Homeland Security and Governmental Affairs
United States Senate

When a contract is set to expire and there is a continuing need for services, but the follow-on contract is not ready to be awarded, the government can extend the existing contract or award a short-term sole-source contract to an incumbent contractor. These types of contracting arrangements have been referred to as "bridge contracts" and are used to ensure there is no gap in services. While bridge contracts can be a necessary and appropriate tool, their use has also been associated with negative effects, such as higher contract prices due to a lack of competition and the inefficient use of staff and resources. For example, contracting officials have to devote their time to awarding a bridge contract while concurrently preparing to award a follow-on contract.

You asked us to assess the use of bridge contracts by federal agencies. This report examines (1) the insights of selected agencies into their use of bridge contracts; (2) key characteristics of selected bridge contracts; and (3) the reasons why bridge contracts are being used.

Since bridge contracts are not identified in the Federal Procurement Data System-Next Generation (FPDS-NG) or any other federal database, to answer these objectives, we developed, for the purposes of this report, a definition of bridge contracts. We also developed a customized search methodology using data from FPDS-NG to identify potential bridge contracts. Our methodology included searching for (1) contract extensions between fiscal years 2010 to 2013 that extended a contract's period of performance and (2) sole-source contracts awarded in fiscal year 2013 that had been awarded to the same contractor by the same contracting organization and for the same services as a preceding contract—and with periods of performance of no more than 12 months. We selected these timeframes so as to increase the likelihood that we could include follow-on contracts in our review. Using the result of this search, we selected three agencies (the Department of Defense (DOD), the Department of Health and Human Services (HHS), and the Department of Justice (DOJ)) and several components within each agency for review, based on those with the highest number of potential bridge contracts. We selected the following eight components for review:

- DOD: Air Force, Army, Navy, and Defense Logistics Agency (DLA)
- HHS: National Institutes of Health (NIH) and Indian Health Service (IHS)
- DOJ: Drug Enforcement Administration (DEA) and Federal Bureau of Prisons (BOP)

To gain insights into the selected agencies' use of bridge contracts, we collected and analyzed any policies and procedures on bridge contracts and interviewed officials about their knowledge of the use of bridge contracts and any management controls that may be in place. Because of its role to provide direction for government-wide procurement policies, regulations, and procedures and to promote economy, efficiency, and effectiveness in government acquisitions, we interviewed staff at the Office of Management and Budget's (OMB) Office of Federal Procurement Policy (OFPP) to discuss their views on the benefits and challenges on the use of bridge contracts. We also used federal internal control standards as criteria for assessing agencies' insights into the use of bridge contracts.[1]

To identify key characteristics of selected bridge contracts and assess the reasons why bridge contracts are being used, we selected a nongeneralizable sample of 73 bridge contracts for services. We focused on service contracts since agency officials and our prior work indicated that bridge contracts were predominantly used for services. We used two processes for identifying the 73 contracts included in our review: (1) 52 contracts identified based on our customized search of FPDS-NG, and (2) 21 contracts initially identified by selected components and verified by us as bridge contracts. To arrive at the selection of the 52 contracts, we provided a list of potential bridge contracts identified through the search methodology described above to each component included in our review. The components then provided contract documentation that we analyzed to determine whether the selected contracts matched our definition of bridge contracts. Based on this analysis, we identified 52 bridge contracts across the components to be included in our review. We then added in 21 contracts identified on lists of bridge contracts provided to us by components included in our review. We conducted a high level review of the 73 contracts—collecting and reviewing contract award and extension documentation, such as justification and approval (J&A) documents, price negotiation memorandums, relevant contract modifications, and file memoranda. We then selected a subset of 29 contracts from 6 of the 8 components for a more in-depth review, based on several factors, specifically the contract value, obtaining a mix of contract extensions and stand-alone bridge contracts, and the location of the contract files.[2] For this in-depth review, we reviewed the bridge contract, the contract preceding it, and, if awarded at the time of our review, the follow-on contract. The results from the sample of contracts included in our review are not generalizable, but are designed to provide illustrative examples of the characteristics and rationale for the use of bridge contracts at the selected agencies and components and supplement the information obtained from our interviews and review of agency policies and procedures. We also interviewed contracting and program officials to discuss the facts and circumstances related to the award of the bridge contracts for the subset of 29 contracts in our sample, and the challenges, if any, related to their use. A more detailed description of our scope and methodology is presented in appendix I.

We conducted this performance audit from June 2014 to October 2015 in accordance with generally accepted government auditing standards. Those standards require that we plan and perform the audit to obtain sufficient, appropriate evidence to provide a reasonable basis for our findings and conclusions based on our audit objectives. We believe that the evidence obtained provides a reasonable basis for our findings and conclusions based on our audit objectives.

BACKGROUND

The federal government contracts for a variety of services, from elevator maintenance to program management support, and often has a need to continue these services beyond the lifespan of an individual contract. However, in certain situations, it may become evident that a base contract and any option years will expire before a subsequent contract to meet the same need can be awarded. In these cases, because of time constraints, contracting officers generally use one of two options: (1) extend the existing contract for up to 6 months or (2) award a short-term stand-alone contract to the incumbent contractor on a sole-source basis to avoid a lapse in services. While these contracting options have been informally referred to as bridge contracts by some in the acquisition community, no formal definition of bridge contracts exists nor is there a requirement to track them in the Federal Acquisition Regulation (FAR). For the purposes of this report, we established the following definitions:

- *Bridge contract.* An extension to an existing contract beyond the period of performance (including option years), or a new, short-term contract awarded on a sole-source basis to an incumbent contractor to avoid a lapse in service caused by a delay in awarding a follow-on contract.
- *Predecessor contract.* The contract in place prior to the award of a bridge contract.
- *Follow-on contract.* A longer-term contract that follows a bridge contract for the same or similar services. This contract can be competitively awarded or awarded on a sole-source basis.

Contract extensions and the award of stand-alone bridge contracts are established in different ways. If a contracting officer needs a bridge contract and opts to extend an existing, predecessor contract, the contracting officer may use a number of different authorities to do this. If the predecessor contract included the "option to extend services clause," the contracting officer could use this clause to extend the contract for up to six months, based on the FAR.[3] If the contracting officer determines that a new short-term sole-source contract should be awarded to avoid a gap in services, the FAR generally requires that the contract award be supported by a written justification known as a justification and approval document (J&A). The J&A must include sufficient facts and rationale to justify the use of a sole-source contract and include, among other things, the following information:

- The nature or description of the action being approved;
- A description of the supplies or services required to meet the agency's need, including the estimated value of the contract;
- The statutory authority being cited to justify a noncompetitive contract—for example urgency, only one-source available, etc;

- A demonstration that the proposed contractor's unique qualifications or the nature of the acquisition requires use of the authority cited; and
- A determination by the contracting officer that the anticipated cost to the government will be fair and reasonable.

While OMB has stated that noncompetitive contracts can play an important role in helping agencies address the needs that arise during emergencies, we and others have noted that competition is the cornerstone of a sound acquisition process and OMB has issued guidelines for federal agencies to increase competition and reduce their spending on sole-source contracts.[4] Further, the FAR prescribes policies and procedures to promote full and open competition.

There are few, if any, federal contracting reviews or reports focused solely on bridge contracts. However, we and others have identified such contracts in prior reviews and, in some cases, reported on challenges related to their use. For instance, in an August 2011 report on acquisition planning, we reported that a prior GAO bid protest decision found that the Department of Homeland Security's U.S. Customs and Border Protection had not properly justified an $11.5 million bridge contract and had failed to engage in reasonable advanced acquisition planning.[5] In a March 2012 report on competition, we found that 18 out of the 111 J&As we reviewed were for bridge contracts with a total value of over $9 billion.[6] We found that these bridge contracts were caused by delays in the acquisition planning process, unexpected expansion of requirements, and bid protests. In March 2014, we issued a report on noncompetitive contracts awarded on the basis of urgency.[7] We found that 12 of the 34 contracts we reviewed were bridge contracts. The average period of performance for these 12 contracts was 11 months with a total contract value over $466 million. Additionally, in a March 2010 report on competition for services contracts, the Institute for Defense Analyses reported that nearly one in four sole-source contracts reviewed were bridge contracts.[8] That report noted that bridge contracts represented a potentially large cost to DOD due to process inefficiencies such as the cost of administering the bridge contracts, the strain on the limited DOD contracting workforce because bridge contracts must be justified and awarded while the follow-on contract was being planned, and the loss of benefits associated with competition during the period that the bridge contracts are in place.

SELECTED AGENCIES HAVE LITTLE TO NO INSIGHT INTO THEIR USE OF BRIDGE CONTRACTS BUT TWO COMPONENTS HAVE INSTITUTED POLICIES

The agencies we reviewed had limited or no insights into their use of bridge contracts. None of the agencies have agency-level policies to manage and track their use of bridge contracts, nor do their acquisition regulations define bridge contracts. HHS officials told us that their agency has no overarching policy because the agency does not have a standard definition for bridge contracts. Officials at DOD said that, at the department-level, the agency did not have any policies because bridge contracts had not previously been raised as a specific concern at the department. DOJ officials indicated they see defining bridge contracts as a government-wide issue, and officials from one of their components told us that the concept of defining bridge contracts was a new one to them.

HHS officials also stated that the agency has some visibility into high-dollar bridge contracts through the FAR-required reviews of J&As.[9]

Two of the eight components—the Navy and DLA—established policies in 2012 and 2013, respectively, regarding the use of bridge contracts. Both components' policies were established to reduce reliance on bridge contracts and note that bridge contracts can be an impediment to competition. DLA's policy further states that bridge contracts may be indicative of a lack of adequate preparation for follow-on acquisitions. DLA officials we spoke with told us that there was concern at DLA regarding the impact bridge contracts could have on competition, since they effectively delay competition by extending existing contracts or awarding sole-source contracts to incumbent contractors. Officials said that they hope the policy will increase competition at DLA by focusing management attention on the use of bridge contracts and tracking their use. In both cases, these components' policies go beyond the standard J&A requirements for sole-source contracts to specifically address bridge contracts. Features of these components' policies on bridge contracts are included in table 1.

As the table shows, DLA's definition of bridge contracts explicitly includes contract extensions whereas the Navy's has additional guidance as to when contract extensions are considered bridges. A DLA official told us that they included contract extensions in their definition because extensions still enable officials to bridge a gap in service without competition.

Table 1. Policies on Bridge Contracts as Instituted at the Navy and DLA

	Navy	*DLA*
Definition	A noncompetitive contract to bridge the time between the end of one contract action and the beginning of another. A subsequent policy memorandum clarifies that if a contract extension is not evaluated at the time of award it shall follow bridge contract procedures.	A noncompetitive contract or order, or an extension to an existing sole-source or competitive contract ororder that is awarded to the existing contractor to bridge the time between the end of the existing contract or order and the award of a follow-on contract or order. The definition of bridge contracts has been incorporated into DLA's Acquisition Directive. This definition indicates that follow-on contract or orders should be competitively awarded.
Approval documents and requirements	•Justification and approvaldocument •Request for authorization to award a bridge contract •Rationale for use of a bridge contract. •Certification of the urgency of the requirement. •Signature of the program manager and the contracting officer.	•Justification and approvaldocument[a] •Request for authorization to award a bridge contract •Explanation as to why the need for a bridge contract is not due to lack of advanced planning or inadequate procurement execution. •Justification for the length of the bridge contract. •Discussion of actions to be taken to avoid additional bridge contracts.
Reporting requirements	•Quarterly to the Office of the Deputy Assistant Secretary of the Navy, Acquisition and Procurement.[b]	•Monthly to the Acquisition Operations Division on bridge contracts greater than $1 billion. •Quarterly to the Acquisition Operations Division on bridge contracts greater than $150,000.

Source: GAO analysis of Navy and DLA documentation. | GAO-16-15.

[a] DLA's policy notes that if a justification and approval document is not required a request for authorization must still be submitted for review and approval.

[b] While not specifically included in the policy, the Office of the Deputy Assistant Secretary of the Navy, Acquisition and Procurement consolidates the data and prepares a "Bridge Report," which is then submitted to the Assistant Secretary of the Navy, Research, Development and Acquisition each quarter.

The Navy report to the Office of the Deputy Assistant Secretary of the Navy, Acquisition and Procurement includes contract numbers, periods of performance for the predecessor and bridge contracts, dollar values, and the rationale supporting the use of a bridge contract, among other information. The DLA report to the Acquisition Operations Division includes contract numbers, periods of performance for the bridge contract, dollar values, number of the bridge contracts awarded for the requirement, and other information.

According to Navy officials, the department is monitoring the contract values of bridge contracts awarded. For example, officials told us that in fiscal year 2014 the Navy made bridge contract awards in excess of $1.6 billion.[10] Navy officials told us that while it is too early to quantify, the implementation of the policy brought about a cultural shift away from more frequent use of bridge contracts and helped significantly curb prolonged use of bridge contracts. According to a DLA official responsible for compiling bridge contract information, DLA awarded $1.3 billion in bridge contract awards in fiscal year 2014. DLA officials also told us that they were seeing reductions in the use of bridge contracts based on an internal review process. Increased attention to bridge contracts, according to a DLA official, sends a message to program-level activities that DLA wants to reduce its use of bridge contracts, and requiring approval appears to be an effective deterrent to awarding bridge contracts if the program or contracting office does not have a good reason to do so, such as poor acquisition planning.[11]

In addition, one activity within the Army—the Health Care Acquisition Activity (HCAA), which was not included as part of our review—issued a policy memorandum in November 2008 that established a definition and an approval and tracking mechanism for bridge contracts. Similar to the policies at the Navy and DLA, HCAA's policy was established due to concern over the increasing reliance on bridge contracts at the activity. In particular, the policy stated that there was concern that bridge contracts, which prevent competition, were being awarded to expand the scope of the original requirement, which was increasing costs. The policy and compliance branch at HCAA developed a tracking system to account for the number of bridge contracts awarded. According to HCAA officials, issuing the policy memorandum and requiring officials to report their use of bridge contracts has enhanced the activity's ability to track bridge contract use and prevented the award of bridge contracts that increase the scope of work established by the predecessor contract.

Federal internal control standards state that agencies should identify, analyze, and monitor risks associated with achieving objectives, and that information needs to be recorded and communicated to management so as to achieve agency objectives.[12] One common procurement objective at federal agencies is to maximize competition. However, without a definition for bridge contracts, and strategies for tracking and managing their use, agencies are not able to fully identify and monitor the risks related to these contracts, and therefore may be missing opportunities to increase competition. As we noted earlier, the FAR does not define bridge contracts. Staff from OMB's OFPP, one of the entities responsible for initiating revisions to the FAR, acknowledged that the use of bridge contracts may introduce risks related to a lack of competition, such as the risk of higher contract prices. Similarly, contracting, program, and policy officials we spoke with also stated that while bridge contracts are an important "tool in their toolbox" for ensuring continuity of services, some officials indicated that their prolonged use poses a risk to competition, and that use of bridge contracts should be avoided when possible.

BRIDGE CONTRACTS COVER A VARIETY OF SERVICES AND CAN SPAN MULTIPLE YEARS, AND FOLLOW-ON CONTRACTS WERE GENERALLY COMPETED

DOD, DOJ, and HHS awarded bridge contracts to procure a diverse array of services, ranging from professional and administrative support to housekeeping. While most of the 73 contracts we reviewed had periods of performance of six months or less, when we did a deeper dive on 29 of these contracts, we found that more than half of these actually had periods of performance far greater than initially apparent. Some spanned several years. Overall, roughly one-third of the 29 contracts had periods of performance that exceeded two years. The increased periods of performance also corresponded to increased contract values. In terms of pricing, contracting officers generally based the prices of bridge contracts we reviewed on historical prices, and our price analysis found some instances of increased prices between the predecessor and bridge contracts. However, even after lengthy bridge contracts, we found that competition occurred in most cases. For 23 of the 26 cases where follow-on contracts were in place, they had been competitively awarded. In some cases, we were able to quantify savings from the competition of the follow-on contracts based on our price analysis. Competition has generally been considered to be associated with achieving more favorable prices, our prior work and those of others has cited potential savings from competition.

Bridge Contracts Are Awarded for a Variety of Services

DOD, DOJ, and HHS awarded bridge contracts for a wide range of services. Figure 1 shows a break-out of the types of services procured through the 73 bridge contracts included in our review.

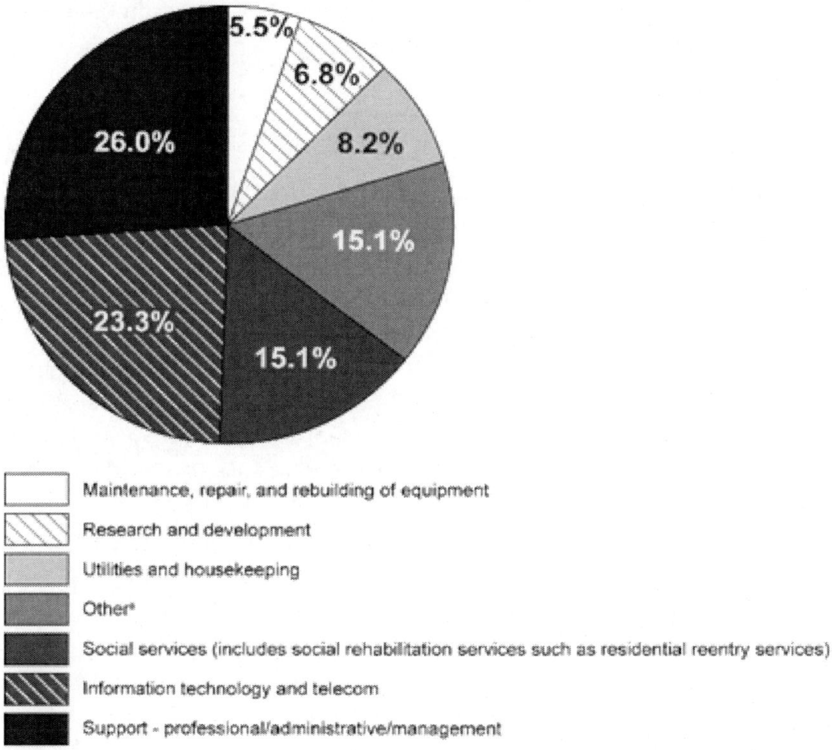

Source: GAO analysis of Federal Procurement Data System – Next Generation data for contracts in our sample. | GAO-16-15.

Figure 1. Types of Services Procured at DOD, DOJ, and HHS for 73 Bridge Contracts.

Over a quarter of the 73 bridge contracts we reviewed were awarded to ensure the continued provision of professional and administrative services, such as the employment of graphic artists and public affairs officers to assist in Navy recruiting efforts, as well as the organization of an NIH-sponsored coalition to adopt nationwide medical imaging standards. Another 23 percent of the bridge contracts we reviewed were awarded for information technology services, including base-wide multimedia and broadcast services for the Army;

text mining software used by NIH officials to categorize and report on research findings; and technology used to track evidence at DEA. Fifteen percent of the bridge contracts were awarded by BOP to provide residential reentry services for eligible inmates, which includes employment, housing, and other opportunities to assist federal offenders' transition back into their communities. Bridge contracts were also awarded for a variety of other services, such as utilities; housekeeping (which runs the gamut from janitorial services to pest control); research and development; and maintenance and repair of equipment or facilities.

Periods of Performance for Many Bridge Contracts Were Longer than Initially Apparent and Spanned Multiple Years

Most of the 73 bridge contracts had periods of performance of less than six months. However, when we conducted our more in-depth review of 29 of these contracts, we found that more than half involved one or more bridges that spanned much longer periods of time. Specifically, we found that 20 of the 29 contracts had additional bridges that were not apparent in our review of the initial documentation, and that more than half of the 29 contracts had periods of performance greater than six months. For example, during our initial review of J&A documentation for an NIH bridge contract for utility services at a research facility, we found no record of an additional four-month bridge contract. Through our interviews with contracting officials, however, we learned that another bridge contract had been awarded prior to the bridge contract we had identified. In another example, our initial review of a J&A for a residential reentry services contract at BOP indicated that contracting officials granted approval for a seven-month bridge contract, but upon further review, we found that there were five separate bridge contracts awarded over a 27- month period between the predecessor and follow-on contracts. Figure 2 depicts the multiple bridges and indicates the 7-month bridge that we had initially identified.

In another example, our initial review of the J&A documentation for an Army bridge contract to procure computer support services indicated that contracting officials had granted approval for a bridge contract that was not to exceed 12 months. However, we later learned from speaking with officials and reviewing additional contract file documentation that the actual period of performance spanned 42 months, as shown in figure 3.

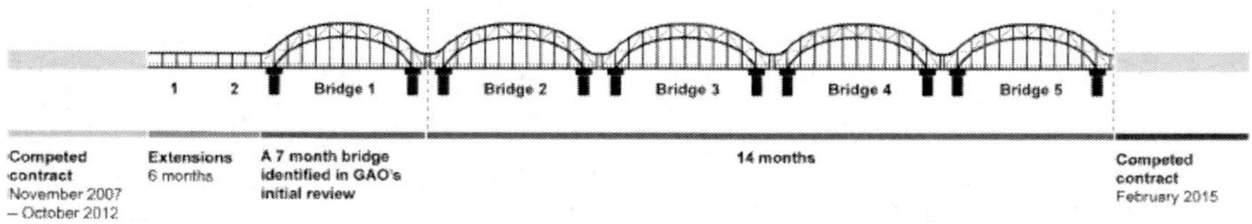

Source: GAO graphic based on information from contract file reviews and interviews with contracting officials. | GAO-16-15.

Figure 2. Timeline for BOP's Residential Reentry Services Contract.

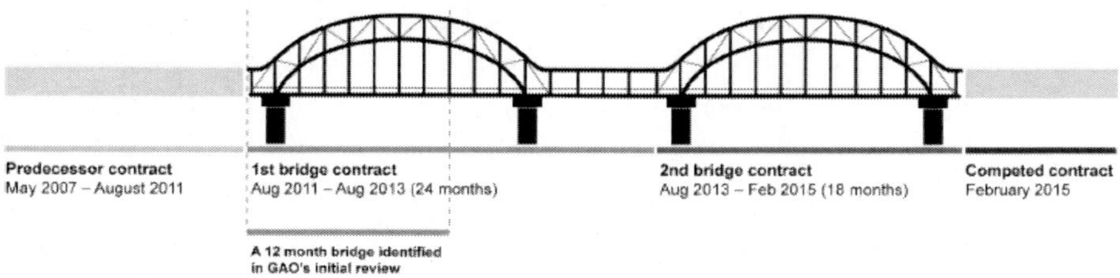

Source: GAO graphic based on information from contract file reviews and interviews with contracting officials. | GAO-16.

Figure 3. Timeline for Army Computer Support Services Contract.

The longer periods of performance observed in our in-depth review corresponded with an increased value of the contracts from what was apparent in our initial review. Most of the 73 contracts included in our high-level review had relatively small dollar values—less than $1 million, while ten percent of the contracts had values greater than $10 million— with the highest valued at $79 million. Our in-depth review, however, revealed the value of the majority of the 29 bridge contracts included in that review to be greater than initially apparent. For example, the J&A for a bridge contract to provide computer support services at the Army awarded to an Alaska Native Corporation—included as a part of our high level review—had an estimate of $20 million. However, based on our in-depth review, the total reported value of the two bridge contracts awarded to bridge the gap in services was over $28 million.[13] In another example, a BOP contract for inmate reentry services, the J&A we initially reviewed estimated the bridge contract value to be about $454,000, but our in-depth review revealed that the value of the five stand-alone bridge contracts awarded for this requirement exceeded $1.2 million. In all, the value of the stand-alone bridge contracts awarded on the contracts we reviewed in-depth was over $225 million.[14]

The fact that the full length of a bridge contract, or multiple bridge contracts for the same requirement, is not readily apparent from the review of an individual J&A presents a challenge for those agency officials responsible for approving the use of bridge contracts. Approving officials, signing off on individual J&As, would not have insight into the total number of bridge contracts that may be put in place by looking at individual J&As alone. Without a definition and a policy for bridge contracts, J&A documentation generally provides information on the individual contract covered by the J&A, and on the anticipated period of performance and estimated contract value at the time of award, rather than a full picture of the cumulative time and cost associated with bridging a gap in services for a requirement.[15]

Overall the average period of performance for the 73 contracts we reviewed at a high-level was 8 months, and the average period of performance for the 29 contracts we reviewed in-depth was 21 months. Figure 4 illustrates that the actual periods of performance for these 29 bridge contracts ranged from two weeks to over five-and-a-half years; about one-third of the contracts had periods of performance that exceeded two years.

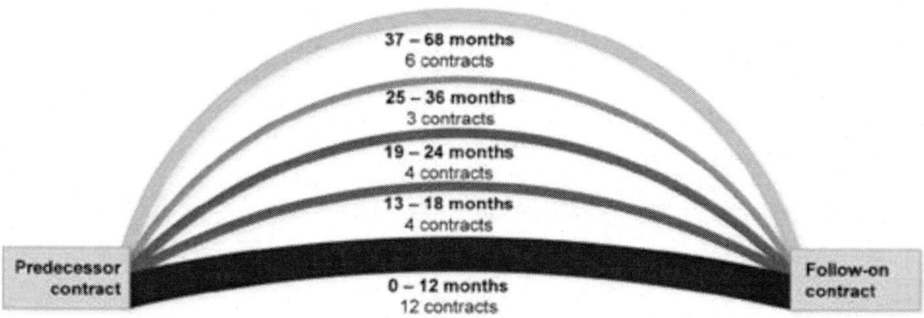

Source: GAO analysis of contract documentation. | GAO-16-15.

Figure 4. Length of Bridge Contracts (29 Contracts Reviewed In-depth).

For 20 bridge contracts included in our in-depth review, contracting officials used the option to extend services clause to bridge, at least in part, the predecessor to the follow-on contract.[16] This clause allows contracting officials to award more than one extension as long as the total period of performance does not exceed six months, but we found that for five of the 29 cases, three of which were in the Army, contracting officials failed to follow the clause in that they had extended the contract beyond the six-month timeframe. For instance, in the example displayed in Figure 3, Army contracting officials extended a bridge contract on two occasions, with each extension lasting six months in duration. This means an additional year was added to the initial period of performance of one year. For both extensions, contracting officials cited the option to extend services clause. Additionally, we learned from contract file review documentation that contracting officials had attempted to extend this bridge contract a third time, but the local office of small business programs denied this request because the incumbent contractor no longer qualified as a small business. Because of the recurring nature of this issue at one location within the Army, we plan to report on the issue separately.

Navy Documentation on Bridge Contracts Tended to Be Relatively More Robust

While Navy bridge contracts spanned similar lengths of time to those of other agencies, we found that the Navy contract files had much more robust documentation and generally identified the reasons for the use of bridge contracts in each J&A. Some of the Navy's J&A documentation included a full account of the length and cost of the bridge contract. For example, the J&A we reviewed for a nine month bridge contract for electromagnetic spectrum management support included the periods of performance for the predecessor contract and one prior bridge contract, and provided a detailed account of the reasons for the delays. In addition, the Navy submitted a follow-on J&A to account for a four-month extension to the bridge contract. The initial J&As listed the value of the bridge contract at almost $4 million. Our in-depth review showed that the combined value of all bridge contracts awarded for this requirement was $4.6 million, which was roughly similar to the estimate provided in the J&As.

J&A documentation we reviewed from other components in our review generally did not detail information on the total cost of the bridge contract in the individual J&A. Further, in some cases, the combined value of the total bridge was more than had been conveyed in an individual J&A. For example, a J&A for a contract to provide scientific, logistical, and administrative support to NIH indicated that a contract extension for six months was estimated to cost $1.5 million. However, our in-depth review of this contract, as well as its predecessor and follow-on contracts, showed that the combined value of all bridge contracts awarded for this requirement was approximately $5 million.

Contracting Officers Cited Historical Price Data in Establishing Fair and Reasonable Prices, and Price Analysis Revealed Some Increased Prices on Bridge Contracts

The FAR requires that contracting officers establish that the prices paid for contracts are fair and reasonable and expresses a preference for comparison of prices obtained through competition. Because competition is absent with the award of a bridge contract, contracting officers' fair and reasonable price determinations become imperative.[17] We were able to collect information on how a contracting officer determined price reasonableness for 73 bridge contracts. Most contracting officials noted that they compared the proposed prices to the historical prices paid for the same or similar services, or used more than one method to establish price reasonableness (see figure 5).

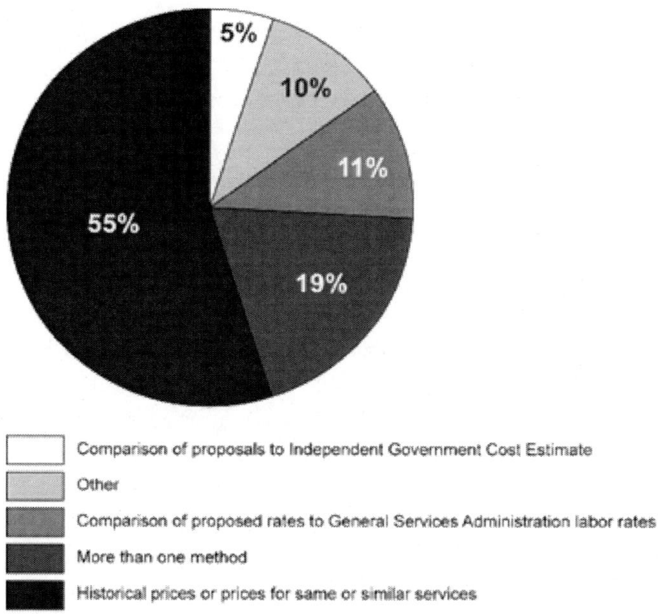

Source: GAO analysis of contract documentation and information provided by agency officials.

Figure 5. Methods Used to Establish Price Reasonableness on 73 Contracts Reviewed.

To determine the extent to which the price paid by the government changed when a bridge contract was awarded to the incumbent contractor for the same services acquired under a previous contract, we conducted a price analysis for 10 of the 29 bridge contracts included in our in-depth review. We compared the rates of selected individual Contract Line Item Numbers (CLIN) for 5 of the 10 bridge contracts to those of their predecessor and competitive follow-on contracts. For 4 of the 10 bridge contracts, which provided residential reentry services to federal inmates, we compared the daily rate paid per inmate, and for the one remaining bridge contract included in this analysis, we compared the hourly price paid for three labor categories to those of the predecessor and follow-on contract. For the remaining 19 contracts we were unable to establish a direct comparison of CLINs or labor categories due to changes to the scope of the requirement or pricing type of the predecessor, bridge, or follow-on contract. Although our analysis was by necessity limited to those CLINs or labor categories that could be traced across the predecessor, bridge, and follow-on contracts, it provided insights into pricing trends for similar services over time.

We found that for 5 of the 10 contracts, the price paid for services on the initial stand-alone bridge contract or contract extension increased from that of the predecessor contract. For example, the monthly rate for administrative and information technology support services increased by nearly $47,000, or 6.4 percent, under a Navy bridge contract, awarded when the predecessor contract expired. However, when the contract was further extended, the price paid decreased by nearly $105,000, or 13.5 percent. Similarly, the CLIN for monthly materials and travel, under a stand-alone Army bridge contract for research and development testing and evaluation services, increased by approximately 5 percent, or $67,400, when compared to the rate of it's predecessor contract. Moreover, when that bridge contract was further extended, the price increased by another 16.6 percent, or $265,000. However, the price paid remained unchanged when the bridge contract was further extended. Of the remaining 5 contracts, in 4 cases the price paid remained the same, and for the remaining contract the price decreased.

Almost All Follow-On Contracts Were Competed, and in Some Cases Savings Could Be Quantified

Follow-on contracts were competitively awarded for 23 of 26 contracts included in our in-depth review.[18] The 3 remaining follow-on contracts were awarded on a sole-source basis.[19] As noted above, competition generally leads to more favorable pricing. The fact that the vast majority of follow-on contracts were competed after the bridge contract expired highlights the urgency of ending bridge contracts as soon as possible, since these contracts are almost always sole-source.[20]

The government has opportunities for savings when the contract awarded following a bridge is competitively awarded. For 7 of the 10 contracts where we conducted a price analysis, savings were achieved upon the award of the follow-on contract. Examples include:

- An Air Force contract for logistic support services that resulted in a monthly rate reduction of approximately $22,400 or 34 percent;
- A daily rate reduction of $10.00 per inmate, or 12.5 percent, for residential reentry services at BOP;
- For a Navy contract providing administrative and professional support services, the rate was reduced by 15.6 percent, or approximately $16 per man hour;

As shown in Figure 6, the hourly rate changed for three labor categories for an Army computer support services contract. While the rate increased from the predecessor contract to the first bridge, it decreased from the first to second bridge, and decreased again from the second bridge to the competitive follow-on contract. Most significant is the rate reduction for the Database Management Specialist; the award of the follow-on contract resulted in a decreased hourly rate of nearly $21.00, or 28 percent. The contracting official responsible for this contract told us that by awarding the follow-on contract competitively, the incumbent contractor had to re-evaluate what price the market demands for these services.

Competition has generally been considered to be associated with achieving more favorable prices, and we and others have cited potential savings from competition in prior work.[21] For example, a 2013 report by the Department of Veterans Affairs' Office of the Inspector General estimated that the Veterans Affairs' Technology Acquisition Center could have saved 20 percent, or approximately $57.9 million, in acquisition costs if task orders for information technology services had been competed.[22]

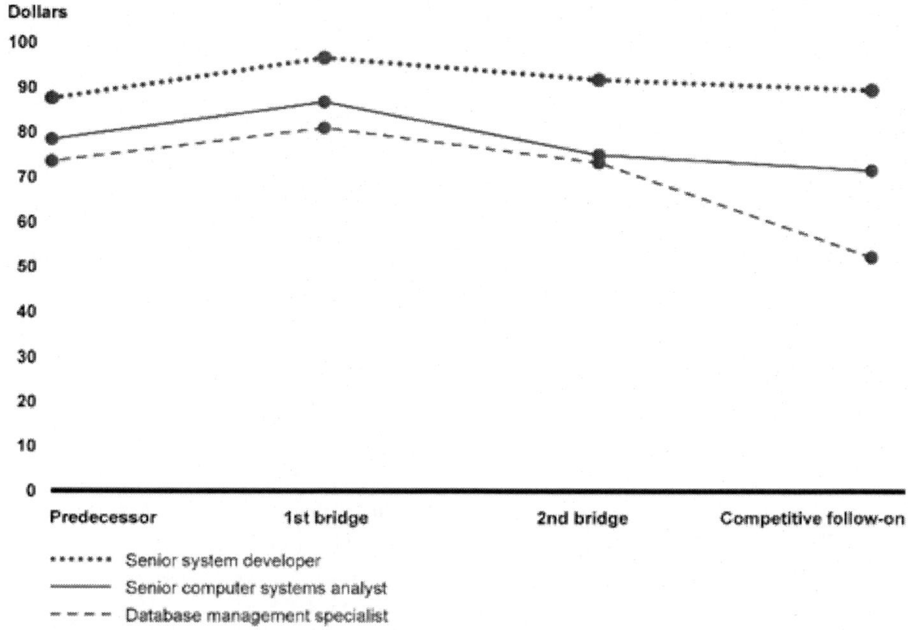

Source: GAO analysis of Army contract documentation. | GAO-16-15.

Figure 6. Hourly Labor Rate Savings for Labor Categories Under an Army Contract for Computer Support Services.

A Variety of Reasons Caused Delays in the Acquisition Process that Led to the Use of Bridge Contracts

A variety of reasons caused delays that resulted in the use of bridge contracts, but late completion of documentation needed to solicit follow-on contracts was the most frequent reason that we identified across our sample of 73 contracts. Contracting officials told us that acquisition workforce problems—such as inexperienced staff and frequent turnover of contracting and program office staff—also led to the use of bridge contracts and influenced other delays, such as late completion of acquisition planning documentation and challenges during source selection. The majority of agency officials that we interviewed identified bid protests as a common reason for the use of bridge contracts, and we found that bid protests had caused delays in eight of the 29 contracts included in our in-depth review–roughly a quarter—

and that bid protests created substantial delays in awarding follow-on contracts.

Late Completion of Acquisition Planning Documentation Most Frequently Identified Reason for Bridge Contracts

Based on our reviews of contract documentation and information provided by agency officials, we found that the most commonly cited reasons for the use of a bridge contract across the 73 contracts were related to acquisition planning issues—in particular the late completion of key acquisition planning documentation, such as statements of work, that are needed to begin a solicitation. Acquisition planning activities generally begin when the program office identifies a need, involves research and preparation of acquisition documents by both the program office and the contracting office, and concludes when the contracting office issues a solicitation. Our prior work has identified challenges that agencies faced in relation to acquisition planning on contracts for services, such as defining their needs and providing guidance to program offices on timeframes for pre-solicitation activities, such as defining requirements in a statement of work document.[23]

Other frequently identified reasons for delays included delays in source selection, acquisition workforce challenges, and bid protests, among others. Figure 7 illustrates the number of instances each reason was cited for the contracts included in our sample. For most of the contracts, there were multiple reasons driving the use of bridge contracts.

Our findings regarding the reasons behind the use of bridge contracts echo the findings of the Institute for Defense Analyses' March 2010 report on competitiveness in contracts for services.[24] That report noted that bridge contracts occur when a delay in the acquisition process prevents the award of a competitive follow-on contract until after the contract in place is due to expire. The report further explained that these delays arise from various sources, including the requiring agency or program office, the contracting office, and other sources such as bid protests.

Our in-depth review of 29 contracts further underscored that acquisition planning issues frequently led to the use of bridge contracts and provided additional insights into the nature of these issues. For example, the majority of the contracting officials that we interviewed cited the late submission of key acquisition planning documentation from program officials as one of the most common reasons why bridge contracts are needed.

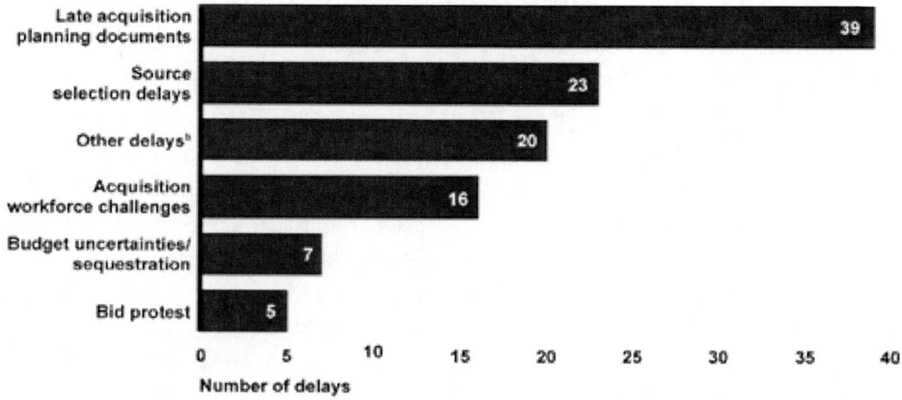

Source: GAO analysis of contact documentation and information provided by agency officials.| GAO-16-15.

[a] In some cases, more than one reason was cited for using a bridge contract. Therefore, the number of reasons exceeds the 73 contracts included in this analysis. Also, for 7 of the 73 contracts included in our high-level review, we were unable to identify the reasons the bridge contract was awarded because officials could not provide information on the reasons for delay.

[b] "Other delays" included contractor related delays, technical challenges with agency databases, introducing new acquisition guidance, contract ceilings that were met prematurely, delays in cost analyses provided by external agencies, termination of previous task orders, and a brief interruption in re-procurement activities. We identified each of these reasons in, at most, 3 contracts reviewed.

Figure 7. Reasons and Timing for Delays Found in High-Level Review of 73 Bridge Contracts.[a]

For 18 of the contracts, contracting officials told us that the statement of work, in particular, was either submitted late by the program office, required multiple rounds of revisions before it was ready to be published, or a combination of those two factors contributed to the need for a bridge contract. Acquisition planning challenges stemming from the coordination of program and contracting offices have been highlighted in some of our past work. For example, in a July 2010 report on competition, we found that several contracting officials from different agencies expressed concern that program offices sometimes do not allow them enough time to execute a sufficiently robust acquisition planning process that could increase opportunities for competition.[25] They told us that program offices are insufficiently aware of the amount of time needed to properly define requirements or conduct adequate market research.

A contract awarded by DEA highlights some of the acquisition planning problems that we found across the 29 contracts. In this example, DEA contracting officials told us that the program office was late in submitting the statement of work. According to those officials, a contract extension was awarded for 6 months to accommodate this delay. During this time, the contracting office issued a solicitation for this requirement and received multiple proposals for the follow-on contract, but the source selection board realized during the proposal evaluation phase that the statement of work did not accurately reflect the agency's needs. Upon realizing that a completely new statement of work was required, DEA decided to cancel the solicitation and awarded a six month bridge contract, which was later extended by three months to accommodate the additional time it needed to award a follow-on contract.

Acquisition planning shortfalls caused substantial delays for some contracts we reviewed at other components as well. For example, at BOP, we found a series of 17 stand-alone bridge contracts, most of which were about three months in length, to provide natural gas service at a penitentiary that were put in place after the predecessor contract expired in January 2011—following a four month contract extension. Contracting officials told us that the program office was extremely late in submitting the necessary paperwork to award a follow-on contract, and did not submit the required acquisition planning documents until February 2014, over three years after the predecessor contract expired. As of the date of this review, contracting officials have yet to award a follow-on contract and attribute these delays to personnel shortages within the contracting office. Specifically, contracting officials told us that they are short-staffed; explaining that 119 different requirements are handled by only two contracting officers, therefore, this requirement often gets placed on the backburner, resulting in the need for bridge contracts to prevent a gap in critical services.

Acquisition Workforce Challenges Also Led to Bridge Contracts

As the previous example highlights, challenges related to the acquisition workforce can exacerbate delays, and thus contribute to the award of bridge contracts. We found that acquisition workforce challenges—in particular, inexperienced and overwhelmed staff, as well as staff turnover—led to the use of bridge contracts and influenced other delays, such as the late completion of acquisition planning documentation and challenges during source selection.

Inexperienced and Overwhelmed Staff

Contracting officials from multiple agencies told us that late statements of work were often a symptom of a lack of knowledgeable and seasoned staff in program offices. For example, contracting and program officials from the Air Force and Army told us that workforce challenges were responsible for inefficiencies or missteps that introduced delays into the acquisition process. Contracting officials at the Air Force told us that in one instance, inexperienced contracting personnel failed to exercise the second annual option for a logistics management contract and the contract expired. However, the contractor continued to provide services during that time without a contract in place for over five weeks before the mistake was realized. As a result of this and other problems, the last two years of the contract could not be used, and a series of noncompetitive bridge contracts totaling 41 months were used until a competitive follow-on contract was awarded. The same Air Force officials also told us that the majority of their contracting workforce had less than five years of experience, which contributed to significant delays in awarding follow-on contracts. Similarly, three Army contracting officials told us that their divisions did not have enough experienced contracting officers or available attorneys to run source-selection boards in order to select vendors for follow-on contracts. One of those officials also told us that their overwhelmed contracting office also struggled to award new contracts in a timely manner. For example, that official told us that a bridge contract that had been in place for 37 months would likely be extended yet again even though it was possible to award a follow-on contract, because it was unclear if anyone in her division would have enough time to dedicate to that requirement before the current bridge contract expired. Contracting and program officials from this Army component concurred that workforce challenges in both the program and contracting offices were the primary reason why they awarded multiple bridge contracts that lasted more than three years. We have found and reported on government-wide acquisition workforce challenges for many years, including DOD's efforts to rebuild the capacity of its acquisition workforce.[26]

Staff Turnover

Contracting and program officials from all three agencies cited staff turnover as another driver of bridge contracts. Specifically, officials told us that turnover contributed to delays for 10 of the 29 bridge contracts in our in-depth sample. In one example, a program official at DEA told us that awarding a follow-on contract for counseling services was delayed in part because there were three different contracting specialists working on the requirement while it was being recompeted. This official also stated that there may have been a larger staffing issue in the contracting office during this time that contributed to the solicitation being issued later than expected after the statement of work had been finalized.

Through our analysis of contract documentation and information provided by agency officials, we also found that a lack of institutional knowledge within the contracting office was apparent for seven of the 73 contracts in our sample. This acquisition workforce problem was generally the result of staff turnover coupled with a lack of contract documentation. For example, after reviewing a contract file for software within DEA laboratories and interviewing contracting and program officials, we were unable to determine the specific reason why a bridge contract was needed. After reviewing the contract documentation following our visit, the DEA was also unable to identify the specific reason for delay that led to a bridge contract. Similarly, DLA could not provide specific reasons beyond the need for continued services for six contracts in our sample. As a point of comparison, the Navy had greater institutional knowledge regardless of staff turnover due to the high level of detail provided in their J&As and contract documentation. Navy officials we spoke with as part of our in-depth review were generally more aware of the facts and circumstances for the bridge contracts they awarded when compared to their counterparts at other components. The contracting officials we spoke with stated that the Navy's policy on bridge contracts has curtailed their use, especially since contracting officials have faced pressure from their superiors to avoid bridge contracts. When bridge contracts are needed, Navy officials said they know a high degree of scrutiny by management will ensue.

Bid Protests Contributed to the Use of Bridge Contracts in Some Cases

The majority of agency officials that we interviewed identified bid protests as a common reason for the use of bridge contracts. While contract documentation cited bid protests as reasons for delay in five of the contracts in our high-level review, when we reviewed the contracts in-depth we found that bid protests caused delays in eight of the 29 contracts—roughly a quarter—and that the protests introduced substantial delays to the acquisition process. For example, NIH received nine protests from the incumbent contractor and other unsuccessful bidders on a requirement for utility maintenance services. In this instance, contracting officers awarded a series of short-term bridge contracts for roughly six years to continue to meet the requirement. Similarly, a BOP contract for residential reentry services received multiple protests that resulted in three stand-alone bridge contracts. The total period of performance for that bridge contract requirement was ultimately 27 months.

In seven of the eight instances of bid protests that we identified, the incumbent contractor protested the award of a follow-on contract to a new vendor or the terms of the solicitation. However, only two of those protests were sustained and resulted in the incumbent receiving the follow-on contract. Most of the losing incumbents were unsuccessful in obtaining follow-on contracts. We also found that as a result of the incumbent's protests, incumbent vendors kept providing services—in a noncompetitive environment—well after the predecessor contracts expired.

The relationship between bridge contracts and bid protests was discussed in a recent U.S. Court of Federal Claims decision. In this decision, the Court discussed BOP's procurement of residential reentry services. In June 2012, BOP issued a Request for Proposals for residential reentry services. During the acquisition process for the follow-on contract, the incumbent's contract for the residential reentry services expired. To avoid a gap in services while completing the acquisition process, BOP awarded—to the incumbent contractor—a total of three stand-alone bridge contracts with a total period of performance of 21 months. During the period of performance of the last bridge, BOP awarded a follow-on contract to a different vendor. The incumbent contractor filed a protest with GAO in April 2015. Rather than enter into a fourth bridge contract with the incumbent contractor, BOP decided to transfer the inmates of the facility being serviced by the incumbent contractor to other facilities. Based on BOP's decision to transfer the inmates, the incumbent filed another protest, this time with the U.S. Court of Federal Claims. The Court denied the incumbent's protest on May 29, 2015.[27]

Contracting Officials Also Cited Budget Uncertainties and Sequestration as Contributing to Bridge Contracts

Contracting officials asserted that budget uncertainty and sequestration contributed to delays in the award of follow-on contracts for four of the 29 contracts that we reviewed in-depth. For example, officials responsible for two Navy contracts—one for information technology and administrative support and the other for information technology and information management—told us that budget uncertainties, including furloughs within their office during the government shutdown in October 2013, contributed to delays in the award of follow-on contracts. They also told us that one program office was unable to commit funding to a full-term contract early enough in the acquisition process to award the follow-on contract in a timely manner. Similarly, BOP officials told us that sequestration cuts resulted in the award of an additional short-term bridge contract for residential reentry services during the shutdown. However, that particular bridge contract was bookended by two extensions to the predecessor and four other bridge contracts that were caused by bid protests and source selection challenges. Overall, the impact of budget uncertainties and sequestration was not immediately clear or quantifiable for any of the contracts in our sample.

CONCLUSION

While bridge contracts can be a useful tool in certain circumstances to avoid a gap in services, they are typically envisioned to be used for short periods of time. When these noncompetitive contracts are used frequently or for prolonged periods of time, the government is at risk of paying more than it should for goods and services. Because we found that almost all of the bridge contracts in our review were ultimately followed by competitive contracts—which can lead to savings for the taxpayer—the importance of awarding these contracts in a timely manner is heightened. By defining bridge contracts and implementing a policy related to their use, the Navy and DLA have taken important steps to enhance these components' management of bridge contracts. However, bridge contracts have been identified not only across the three agencies and eight components included in our review, but at other agencies as well, as evidenced by our past work and that of others. Therefore, the importance of defining and tracking bridge contracts is not limited to those agencies included in our review. A uniform, government-wide definition and strategies for tracking and managing the use of bridge contracts would help ensure all agencies have better insights into their use of these contracts and provide agencies with the information necessary to manage their use. Otherwise, agencies are left without a complete picture or understanding of how long a bridge contract has been in place. Without such information, it is difficult for agencies to take steps to reduce their reliance on noncompetitive bridge contracts or remediate internal deficiencies—such as issues related to acquisition planning or challenges with the acquisition workforce—that may lead to delays in the award of follow-on contracts.

RECOMMENDATIONS FOR EXECUTIVE ACTION

To gain visibility and enable efficient management on the use of bridge contracts in federal agencies, we recommend that the Administrator of OFPP take the following two actions:

1. Take appropriate steps to develop a standardized definition for bridge contracts and incorporate it as appropriate into relevant FAR sections, and
2. As an interim measure, until the FAR is amended, provide guidance to agencies on
    - a definition of bridge contracts, with consideration of contract extensions as well as stand-alone bridge contracts; and
    - suggestions for agencies to track and manage their use of these contracts, such as identifying a contract as a bridge in a J&A when it meets the definition, and listing the history of previous extensions and stand-alone bridge contracts back to the predecessor contract in the J&A.

AGENCY COMMENTS AND OUR EVALUATION

We provided a draft of this report to OMB, DOD, HHS, and DOJ for review and comment. DOD and DOJ provided technical comments which we incorporated as appropriate. HHS had no comments.

In an email response, OMB's OFPP concurred with our recommendation to provide guidance to agencies on bridge contracts. With regard to our recommendation to develop a definition of bridge contracts and incorporate it in the FAR, OFPP stated its intention to work with members of the FAR Council to explore the value of doing so. Specifically, OFPP stated it agreed with our conclusion that heightened management attention on bridge contracts can help to remediate weaknesses that may sometimes cause protracted reliance on incumbent contractors after contract expiration. The response further stated that, for this reason, OFPP generally concurs with the recommendation to issue guidance and increase agency attention on these vehicles. It noted that while there is a legitimate role for bridge contracts in helping to avoid lapses in service that can cause mission harm, agencies bear a responsibility, as a part of effective risk management, to ensure this authority is being used only to the extent necessary and in accordance with FAR requirements that are designed to promote competition, including limitations on extensions and execution of justifications and approvals when competition is not used. OFPP stated that it intends to work with the members of the FAR Council and U.S. Chief Acquisition Officer's Council to review relevant FAR coverage and discuss the value of developing a regulatory definition for a bridge contract or making other refinements to address non-competitive work with incumbent contractors beyond the period of contract performance. We appreciate that OFPP will be taking steps to explore the option of adding a definition into the FAR, and we continue to believe that a uniform, government-wide definition for bridge contracts is imperative to providing agencies with the information necessary to monitor these contracts and to ensure they are being used as intended.

Michele Mackin, Director
Acquisition and Sourcing Management

APPENDIX I: OBJECTIVES, SCOPE, AND METHODOLOGY

Our report examines (1) the insights of selected agencies into their use of bridge contracts; (2) key characteristics of selected bridge contracts; and (3) the reasons why bridge contracts are being used. Since bridge contracts are not defined by the Federal Acquisition Regulation (FAR), we, in consultation with our general counsel, developed a definition for bridge contracts based on our prior reviews and knowledge of bridge contracts and the Institute for Defense Analyses report on competition for service contracts—which defined bridge contracts.[1] For the purposes of this report, we established the following definitions:

- *Bridge contract.* An extension to an existing contract beyond the period of performance (including option years), or a new, short-term contract awarded on a sole-source basis to an incumbent contractor to avoid a lapse in service caused by a delay in awarding a follow-on contract.
- *Predecessor contract.* The contract in place prior to the award of a bridge contract.

- *Follow-on contract.* A longer-term contract that follows a bridge contract for the same or similar services. This contract can be competitively awarded or awarded on a sole-source basis.

Since bridge contracts are not identified in any federal database, to select agencies and components for our review, we developed a customized search methodology using data from the Federal Procurement Data System-Next Generation (FPDS-NG) to identify potential bridge contracts. Details on this customized methodology are outlined in a separate section below. Using the results of the customized methodology, we selected three agencies (the Departments of Defense (DOD), Health and Human Services (HHS), and Justice (DOJ)) and eight components within those agencies for review. The selected components were as follows:

- DOD: Air Force, Army, Navy, and Defense Logistics Agency (DLA)
- HHS: National Institutes of Health (NIH) and Indian Health Service (IHS)
- DOJ: Drug Enforcement Administration (DEA) and Federal Bureau of Prisons (BOP)

To gain insights into the selected agencies' use of bridge contracts, we collected and analyzed policies and procedures on bridge contracts in place at the selected agencies and components. We interviewed acquisition and contracting officials about their knowledge of the use of bridge contracts and any management controls, such as tracking or approval processes, in place in relation to bridge contracts. Because of its role in providing direction for government-wide procurement policies, regulations and procedures, and to promote economy, efficiency, and effectiveness in government acquisitions, we also interviewed staff at the Office of Management and Budget's Office of Federal Procurement Policy (OFPP) to discuss their views on the benefits and challenges on the use of bridge contracts. We also used federal internal control standards as criteria for assessing agencies' insights into the use of bridge contracts.[2]

To identify key characteristics of selected bridge contracts and assess the reasons why bridge contracts are being used, we selected 73 bridge contracts across the eight components to be included in our high level review, and a subset of 29 of those contracts to be included in our more in-depth review. The selection process for the contracts is described in detail below. For our high level review, we collected and analyzed contract documentation for the 73 bridge contracts, such as justification and approval (J&A) documents, contract modifications, price negotiation memorandums, and other key file documentation used to support the award of a stand-alone bridge contract or contract extension. We analyzed this information to identify key characteristics of the bridge contracts, such as the period of performance and the authority used to extend the existing contract or award the stand-alone contract. In addition, we reviewed information in FPDS-NG on these 73 contracts to identify the types of services procured and the contract value.[3] To identify the reasons for the award of the bridge contract and the methods used to determine price reasonableness across the 73 contracts, we analyzed the contract file documentation and, in situations where the contract file documentation did not include information on the reason for award or the methods used to determine price reasonableness, we followed up with agency officials. To gain additional knowledge about the facts and circumstances surrounding the award of bridge contracts, we conducted an in-depth review of the subset of 29 contracts. For the in-depth review, we conducted site visits to six locations selected based on the location of contract files, collected and analyzed contract documentation from the predecessor contract, bridge contract(s), and, if awarded at the time of our review, the follow-on contract, and conducted interviews with contracting and program officials for each contract. We analyzed the contract documentation and the interviews to develop a more in-depth understanding of certain characteristics of bridge contracts, such as the length of time between the end of the predecessor contract and the award of the follow-on contract, the extent to which follow-on contracts were competed, and the change in prices between the predecessor, bridge, and follow-on contracts. To determine the extent to which the price paid by the government changed when a bridge contract was awarded to the incumbent contractor for the same services acquired under a previous contract, we conducted a price analysis for 10 of the 29 bridge contracts included in our in-depth review. We compared the rates of individual Contract Line Item Numbers (CLIN) for 5 of these bridge contracts, their predecessor, and competitive follow-on. For 4 of these bridge contracts, which provide residential reentry services to federal inmates, we compared the daily rate paid per inmate, and for the remaining bridge contract included in our analysis, we compared the hourly price paid for three labor categories, commonly referred to as labor rates.[4] The remaining 19 contracts included in our in-depth review were excluded from our price analysis as we were unable to compare these contracts due to changes to the scope of the requirement or pricing type of the predecessor, bridge, or follow-on contract. Although our analysis was by necessity limited to those CLINs or labor categories that could be traced across the predecessor, bridge, and follow-on contracts, it provided insights into pricing trends for similar services over time.

We also analyzed the contract documentation and our interviews with contracting and program officials to develop a more in-depth understanding of the reasons for the award of bridge contracts.

Methodology for Selection of Agencies and Components

Since bridge contracts are not identified in FPDS-NG or any other federal database, to select agencies and components for our review, we developed a customized search methodology using data from FPDS-NG to identify potential bridge contracts. We initially searched for the term "bridge contracts" in the description field of FPDS-NG for contracts awarded in fiscal year 2013. We excluded contracts for physical bridges (i.e., structures that carry a pathway or roadway over a gap or barrier). This search yielded a total of 11 bridge contracts. Given the small number of contracts that this search yielded, we developed a customized search methodology using FPDS-NG data fields so as to increase our chances of obtaining a larger data set of potential bridge contracts. Our customized search was based on our definition of bridge contracts and included searches for both extensions to existing contracts and stand-alone bridge contracts:

- *Extensions.* To find extensions to existing contracts, we searched FPDS-NG for sole-source and competitive contracts awarded between fiscal year 2010 and 2013 where the current completion date was later than the initial completion date. We excluded annual contract options, contract closeouts, and terminations from this search.
- *Stand-alone bridge contracts.* To find potential stand-alone bridge contracts, we searched for contracts awarded in fiscal year 2013 that met the following characteristics:
  - Sequentially awarded contracts (within 90 days) by the same component and contracting organization, at the same location, to the same contractor, for the same services.
  - The second of the sequentially awarded contracts was sole-source and had a period of performance of 12 months or less.

We selected the years 2010-2013 so as to increase the likelihood that a follow-on contract had been awarded subsequent to the bridge contracts, and could therefore be included in our review. Using this methodology, we arrived at the selection of the three agencies and eight components identified earlier in the appendix. We selected the agencies and components with consideration of the fact they were among those with the highest number of potential bridge contracts, and with consideration of on-going work we had at those entities.[5]

We developed a nongeneralizable sample of 73 bridge contracts for services. We focused on service contracts since agency officials and our prior work indicated that bridge contracts were predominantly for services. We used two processes for identifying the 73 contracts included in our review: (1) 52 contracts were identified through our customized search of FPDS-NG, and (2) 21 contracts were initially identified by selected components and verified by us as bridge contracts.

Using the results of the FPDS-NG customized search methodology previously described, we selected contracting offices within the components reviewed based on the number of potential bridge contracts and the location of the contracting offices. We compiled a list of approximately 600 potential bridge contracts from these contracting offices. In selecting these potential bridge contracts, we aimed to ensure that there was a mix of contract extensions and stand-alone bridge contracts. We excluded contracts that had contract values below the simplified acquisition threshold of $150,000, as these contracts are generally exempt from the competition requirements of the FAR.[6] We provided the lists of contracts to each component in our review and asked them to provide contract award and extension documentation, such as J&A documents and contract modifications, to verify whether or not the contracts met our definition of a bridge contract. We excluded some potential bridge contracts with certain features for the purposes of this report.[7] At the end of this process, we had identified 52 contracts as bridge contracts to be included in our review.

In addition, we selected 21 contracts—12 from DLA and 9 from NIH—from agency lists of bridge contracts that these two components had provided us at the beginning of the review. These contracts were either awarded, in progress of being awarded, or extended in fiscal year 2013 or fiscal year 2014. With the addition of these 21 contracts, our sample for our high level review totaled 73 bridge contracts. See table 2 for a break out of the contracts in our sample.

Table 2. Number of Bridge Contracts Included in High Level Review by Component

Component	Number of Bridge Contracts
Army	10
Air Force	3
Navy	14
DLA	12
BOP	14
DEA	5
NIH	13
IHS	2
Total	73

Source: GAO analysis of agencies' contract documentation. | GAO-16-15.

To gain additional knowledge as to the facts and circumstances surrounding the award of bridge contracts, we selected a subset of 29 of the 73 contracts from 6 of the 8 components for a more in-depth review. [8]

These 29 contracts were selected based on several factors, specifically contract value, obtaining a mix of contract extensions and stand-alone bridge contracts, and the location of the contract files.

The sample of contracts included in our review is not generalizable to a larger universe, but is designed to provide illustrative examples of the characteristics and rationale for the use of bridge contracts at the selected agencies and components, and supplement the information obtained from our interviews and review of agency policies and procedures.

We conducted this performance audit from June 2014 to October 2015 in accordance with generally accepted government auditing standards. Those standards require that we plan and perform the audit to obtain sufficient, appropriate evidence to provide a reasonable basis for our findings and conclusions based on our audit objectives. We believe that the evidence obtained provides a reasonable basis for our findings and conclusions based on our audit objectives.

End Notes

[1] GAO, Internal Control: Standards for Internal Control in the Federal Government, GAO/AIMD-00-21.3.1 (Washington D.C.: November 1999).

[2] We excluded DLA and IHS from our in-depth review of 29 contracts. IHS was excluded due to the limited number of contracts verified as bridge contracts and DLA was excluded so as to maintain a balance in the number of contracts across the three agencies included in the review. While we did not include contracts from DLA in our in-depth review, we did include contracts from DLA in our higher level review, and we talked to DLA officials about their insights into bridge contracts and the policies and procedures they have put in place for management oversight.

[3] FAR § 17.208(f) provides for the use of the clause cited at FAR § 52.217-8, "Option to Extend Services" in solicitations and contracts for services when the inclusion of an option is appropriate. This option provision may be exercised more than once, but the total extension of performance shall not exceed 6 months.

[4] See, for example, GAO, Federal Contracting: Opportunities Exist to Increase Competition and Assess Reasons When Only One Offer is Received, GAO-10-833 (Washington, D.C.: July 26, 2010); and OMB/OFPP, Memorandum for Chief Acquisition Officers and Senior Procurement Executives, Subject: Increasing Competition and Structuring Contracts for Best Results (October 27, 2009).

[5] GAO, Acquisition Planning: Opportunities to Build Strong Foundations for Better Service Contracts, GAO-11-672 (Washington, D.C.: August 9, 2011), and see VSE Corp.; Johnson Control World Servs., B-290452.3, May 23, 2005, 2005 CPD ¶ 103.

[6] GAO, Defense Contracting: Competition for Services and Recent Initiatives to Increase Competitive Procurements, GAO-12-384 (Washington, D.C.: March 15, 2012).

[7] GAO, Federal Contracting: Noncompetitive Contracts Based on Urgency Need Additional Oversight, GAO-14-304 (Washington, D.C.: March 26, 2014).

[8] Institute for Defense Analyses, Competitiveness in the Service Sector, IDA Paper P4542 (Alexandria, Va.: March 2010).

[9] The FAR requires that all agencies submit J&As for higher level review for contracts above certain dollar thresholds.

[10] Navy officials noted that these numbers are based in part on ceiling values, and includes contracts awarded to multiple vendors.

[11] DLA policy identifies four reasons where the use of a bridge contract is considered valid, such as when a competitive follow-on contract or solicitation has been protested, or when an approved acquisition strategy requires a change and is endorsed by the head of the contracting activity.

[12] GAO/AIMD-00-21.3.1.

[13] Our prior work on Alaska Native Corporations and other tribal firms under the 8(a) small business set-aside program has discussed issues related to competitive and sole-source procurements. See for example, GAO, Federal Contracting: Monitoring and Oversight of 8(a) Tribal Firms Needs Attention, GAO-12-84 (Washington, D.C.: January 31, 2012) and GAO, Contract Management: Increased Use of Alaska Native Corporation's Special 8(a) Provisions Calls for Tailored Oversight, GAO-06-399 (Washington, D.C.: April 27, 2006).

[14] The $225 million includes stand-alone bridge contracts for 20 of the 29 contracts we reviewed in-depth. The other 9 contracts used only contract extensions to bridge the gap in services. Fourteen of the 29 contracts used a combination of stand-alone bridge contracts and contract extensions. We were unable to calculate the value of contract extensions, as these values are reported as part of the predecessor contract in FPDS-NG.

[15] In our report on noncompetitive contracts awarded based on urgency, we recommended that the agencies we reviewed develop an oversight mechanism when the cumulative value of noncompetitive contracts awarded on the basis of unusual and compelling urgency increases

considerably beyond the initial contract award value. The agencies generally agreed with our recommendations. GAO, Federal Contracting: Noncompetitive Contracts Based On Urgency Need Additional Oversight, GAO-14-304 (Washington, D.C.: March 26, 2014).

[16] FAR § 17.208(f) provides for the use of FAR clause 52.217-8, "Option to Extend Services" in solicitations and contracts for services when the inclusion of an option is appropriate. This provision may be exercised more than once, but the total extension of performance shall not exceed 6 months.

[17] The FAR lists several methods that could help establish price reasonableness in the absence of competition, such as conducting market research or comparing pricing to historical price data. FAR § 15.404-2.

[18] Out of the 29 contracts we reviewed in-depth, three follow-on contracts had not been awarded during the time of our review. Of these, one was awaiting a sole-source award and the other two were planned for competition.

[19] Fifteen of the 26 follow-on contracts were awarded to the incumbent contractor.

[20] Contract extensions that used FAR clause 52.217-8, "Option to Extend Services" are considered to be competitive if the option was evaluated at the time of contract award. FAR §§ 17.206(a) and 17.208 (f).

[21] For example, see GAO-10-833 and GAO-12-384.

[22] Department of Veterans Affairs: Office of the Inspector General's Audit on the Technology Acquisition Center Contract Operations, 12-02387-343, September 27, 2013.

[23] GAO-11-672.

[24] Institute for Defense Analyses, Competitiveness in the Service Sector, IDA Paper P-4542 (Alexandria, Va.: March 2010).

[25] GAO-10-833.

[26] For example, see GAO, Acquisition Workforce: DOD's Efforts to Rebuild Capacity Have Shown Some Progress, GAO-12-232T (Washington, D.C.: November 16, 2011); GAO, Department of Homeland Security: A Strategic Approach is Needed to Better Ensure the Acquisition Workforce Can Meet Mission Needs, GAO-09-30 (Washington, D.C.: November 19, 2008); and GAO, Acquisition Workforce: Status of Agency Efforts to Address Future Needs, GAO-03-55 (Washington, D.C.: December 18, 2002).

[27] Bannum Inc. v. U.S. 121 Fed. Cl. 543 (2015).

End Notes for Appendixd I

[1] Institute for Defense Analyses, Competitiveness in the Service Sector, IDA Paper P4542, (Alexandria, Va.: March 2010).

[2] GAO, Internal Control: Standards for Internal Control in the Federal Government, GAO/AIMD-00-21.3.1 (Washington D.C.: November 1999).

[3] We reported the contract value based on the base and all options value, as reported in FPDS-NG.

[4] We compared the last rate of the predecessor contract to the first rate paid of the bridge contract. We then compared the last rate of the bridge contract to the first rate of the follow-on contract. We used this methodology rather than compare a contract's average rate.

[5] For example, we did not select the Department of Veterans Affairs for our review because we had ongoing work on the contracting practices at this agency. We have since completed that

review. See GAO, Veterans Affairs Contracting: Improved Oversight Needed for Certain Contractual Arrangements, GAO-15-581 (Washington D.C.: July 2, 2015).

[6] See FAR § 6.001(a).

[7] For example, we excluded classified contracts so as to maintain an unclassified report, and contract extensions used to accommodate construction change orders because these extensions are not due to a delay in the award of a follow-on contract.

[8] We excluded DLA and IHS from our in-depth review of 29 contracts. IHS was excluded due to the limited number of contracts verified as bridge contracts. We excluded DLA so as to maintain a balance in the number of contracts across the three agencies included in the review (i.e., since Army, Navy, and Air Force were included in the review as DOD components, we did not include DLA in the in-depth review so as not to have a much larger number of contracts from DOD components than from DOJ or HHS components). While we did not include contracts from DLA in our in-depth review, we did include contracts from DLA in our higher level review, and we talked to DLA officials about their insights into bridge contracts and the policies and procedures they have put in place for management oversight. In addition, for one bridge contract we had initially identified based on an extension, we also included a stand-alone contract awarded prior to the extension as a part of the total bridge. While the bridge contract portion of the requirement did not fully meet our definition of a bridge contract because it was not awarded to the incumbent contractor, we included it as a part of the bridge because it was labeled as a bridge in the file documentation and Army officials told us that it served to bridge the gap in services until a competitive follow-on was awarded. The length of the contract was 12 months and the subsequent extensions totaled 12 months.

In: Noncompetitive Federal Contracting ISBN: 978-1-63485-153-4
Editor: Janet Weaver

Chapter 2

FEDERAL CONTRACTING: NONCOMPETITIVE CONTRACTS BASED ON URGENCY NEED ADDITIONAL OVERSIGHT*

United States Government Accountability Office

WHY GAO DID THIS STUDY

Competition is a critical tool for achieving the best return on the government's investment. Federal agencies are generally required to award contracts competitively but are permitted to award noncompetitive contracts under certain circumstances, such as when requirements are of such an unusual and compelling urgency that the government would suffer serious financial or other injury. Contracts that use the urgency exception to competition must generally be no longer than one year in duration.

The conference report for the National Defense Authorization Act of Fiscal Year 2013 mandated GAO to examine DOD's, State's, and USAID's use of this exception. For the three agencies, GAO assessed (1) the pattern of use, (2) the reasons agencies awarded urgent noncompetitive contracts and the extent to which justifications met FAR requirements; and (3) the extent to which agencies limited the duration. GAO analyzed federal procurement data, interviewed contracting officials, and analyzed a non-generalizable sample of

* This is an edited, reformatted and augmented version of a United States Government Accountability Office, Publication No. GAO-14-304, dated March 2014.

62 contracts with a mix of obligation levels and types of goods and services procured across the three agencies.

WHAT GAO RECOMMENDS

GAO recommends that DOD, State and USAID provide guidance to improve data reliability and oversight for contracts awarded using the urgency exception. GAO also recommends that OFPP provide clarifying guidance to ensure consistent implementation of regulations. Agencies generally agreed with the recommendations.

WHAT GAO FOUND

The Departments of Defense (DOD) and State and the U.S. Agency for International Development (USAID) used the urgency exception to a limited extent, but the reliability of some federal procurement data elements is questionable. For fiscal years 2010 through 2012, obligations reported under urgent noncompetitive contracts ranged from less than 1 percent to about 12 percent of all noncompetitive contract obligations. During that time, DOD obligated $12.5 billion noncompetitively to procure goods and services using the urgency exception, while State and USAID obligated $582 million and about $20 million respectively, almost exclusively to procure services. Among the items procured were personal armor, guard services and communications equipment to support missions in Afghanistan and Iraq. GAO found coding errors that raise concerns about the reliability of federal procurement data on the use of the urgency exception. Nearly half—28 of the 62 contracts in GAO's sample—were incorrectly coded as having used the urgency exception when they did not. GAO found that 20 of the 28 miscoded contracts were awarded using procedures that are more simple and separate from the requirements related to the use of the urgency exception. Ensuring reliability of procurement data is critical as these data are used to inform procurement policy decisions and facilitate oversight.

For the 34 contracts in GAO's sample that were properly coded as having used the urgency exception, agencies cited a range of urgent circumstances, primarily to meet urgent needs for combat operations or to avoid unanticipated gaps in program support. The justifications and approvals—which are required by the Federal Acquisition Regulation (FAR) to contain certain facts and rationale to justify use of the urgency exception to competition—generally contained the required elements; however, some were ambiguous about the specific risks to the government if the acquisition was delayed.

Ten of the 34 contracts in GAO's sample had a period of performance of more than one year—8 of which were modified after award to extend the period of performance beyond 1 year. The FAR limits contracts using the urgency exception to one year in duration unless the head of the agency or a designee determines that exceptional circumstances apply. Agencies did not make this determination for the 10 contracts. The FAR is not clear about what steps agencies should take when a contract is modified after award to extend the period of performance over 1 year. Some contracting officials noted that these modifications are treated as separate contract actions and would not require the determination by the head of the agency or designee. Others considered them cumulative actions requiring the determination. *Standards for Internal Controls in the Federal Government* calls for organizations to maintain proper controls that ensure transparency and accountability for stewardship of government resources. The Office of Federal Procurement Policy (OFPP)—which provides governmentwide policy on federal contracting procedures—is in a position to clarify when the determination of exceptional circumstances is needed to help achieve consistent implementation of this requirement across the federal government. Further, under the urgency exception, the FAR requires agencies to seek offers from as many vendors as practicable given the circumstances. For some contracts in GAO's sample, lack of access to technical data rights and reliance on contractor expertise prevented agencies from obtaining competition.

ABBREVIATIONS

AFRL	Air Force Research Laboratory
DLA	Defense Logistics Agency
DOD	Department of Defense
FAR	Federal Acquisition Regulation
FPDS-NG	Federal Procurement Data System-Next Generation
IED	improvised explosive device
ISR	intelligence, surveillance and reconnaissance
OFPP	Office of Federal Procurement Policy
OMB	Office of Management and Budget

PGSS	Persistent Ground Surveillance System
PTDS	Persistent Threat Detection System
State	Department of State
USAID	U.S. Agency for International Development

* * *

March 26, 2014

Congressional Committees

In fiscal year 2013, the federal government obligated more than $459 billion to procure goods and services, of which approximately $164 billion—about 36 percent—were not competed. Competition in contracting is a critical tool for achieving the best return on investment for taxpayers and can help save the taxpayer money, improve contractor performance, and promote accountability for results. While federal statute and acquisition regulations generally require that contracts be awarded on the basis of full and open competition, they also allow agencies to award noncompetitive contracts in certain circumstances. For example, when the agency's need for goods and services is of an unusual and compelling urgency that precludes full and open competition, agencies may be permitted to award noncompetitive contracts where a delay in award would result in serious financial or other injury to the government. Nonetheless, the Federal Acquisition Regulation (FAR) pertaining to the award of a noncompetitive contract on the basis of urgency requires that agencies request offers from as many sources as is practicable given the circumstances; however, agencies may limit the number of sources from which it solicits offers.[1]

Promoting competition—even in a limited form—increases the potential for quality goods and services at a lower price in urgent situations. Past GAO work has found that the federal government may realize significant cost savings when awarding contracts competitively. In fiscal year 2013, the federal government obligated about $3 billion through noncompetitive contracts on the basis of a compelling urgency to procure goods and services. Noncompetitive contracts carry the risk of overspending because, among other things, they have been negotiated without the benefit of competition, to help establish pricing; one way to mitigate risk is to limit the contract's performance period. In 2009, a new requirement was included in the FAR that, among other things, limits the period of performance for contracts awarded noncompetitively on the grounds of urgency to no longer than 1 year unless there is a determination that exceptional circumstances apply.[2]

The conference report for the National Defense Authorization Act for Fiscal Year 2013 mandated that GAO review the use of the unusual and compelling urgency exception to full and open competition by the Departments of Defense (DOD) and State and the U.S. Agency for International Development (USAID).[3] This report addresses: (1) the pattern of DOD's, State's, and USAID's use of the unusual and compelling urgency exception, including the range of goods and services acquired; (2) the reasons that agencies awarded noncompetitive contracts on the basis of urgency, and the extent to which justifications met requirements in the FAR; and (3) the extent to which agencies limited the duration of the contract and achieved competition in urgent situations.

To determine patterns of DOD's, State's, and USAID's use of the unusual and compelling urgency exception to competition, we analyzed data from the Federal Procurement Data System-Next Generation (FPDS-NG) for fiscal years 2010 through 2012, which represented the time period after the duration requirement went into effect and reflected the most current data to show trends over time. We determined that the federal procurement data were sufficiently reliable to identify these three agencies' use of the urgency exception, in part by verifying a non-generalizable random sample of the data and adjusting the data to account for known limitations by limiting our analysis to the procurement data we could reasonably confirm were awarded using the urgency exception. To determine the reasons that agencies awarded noncompetitive contracts on the basis of urgency and the extent to which justifications met FAR requirements, we used federal procurement data to select a non-generalizable sample of 62 contract files based on largest obligations and a mix of products and services contracts. We analyzed justifications and other documents agencies used to seek approval to limit competition on the selected contracts to identify agencies' rationale for using the urgency exception and determined whether they met FAR requirements. We conducted legal research, analyzed DOD, State, and USAID policies and guidance, and interviewed officials on use of the urgency exception. We compared agencies' policies and procedures with the *Standards for Internal Control in the Federal Government* which calls for documenting transactions to provide evidence of implementation.[4] To determine the extent to which agencies complied with the FAR requirement to limit the contract period and obtained competition, we performed an in depth review of contract files for 34 selected contracts that we identified from our sample of 62 contracts were awarded using the unusual and compelling urgency exception. In addition, we spoke with officials from the Office of Federal Procurement Policy (OFPP) in the Office of Management and Budget (OMB)—which has responsibility for federal procurement policy—about agencies' approaches to implement the FAR requirement to limit the period of performance for contracts awarded under the urgency exception. We compared agencies' approaches to implement the FAR requirement to limit the period of performance with *Standards for Internal Control in the Federal Government* which calls for organizations to maintain proper controls to ensure transparency and accountability for stewardship of resources.[5]

A more detailed description of our scope and methodology is presented in appendix I. We conducted this performance audit from March 2013 through March 2014 in accordance with generally accepted government auditing standards. Those standards require that we plan and perform the audit to obtain sufficient, appropriate evidence to provide a reasonable basis for our findings and conclusions based on our audit objectives. We believe that the evidence obtained provides a reasonable basis for our findings and conclusions based on our audit objectives.

BACKGROUND

Agencies are generally required to use full and open competition—achieved when all responsible sources are permitted to compete—when awarding contracts. However, the Competition in Contracting Act of 1984 recognizes that full and open competition is not feasible in all circumstances and authorizes contracting without full and open competition under certain conditions.[6] Examples of allowable exceptions to full and open competition include circumstances when the contractor is the only source capable of performing the work or when disclosure of the agency's need would compromise national security. An agency may also award a contract noncompetitively when the need for goods and services is of such an unusual and compelling urgency that the federal government faces the risk of serious financial or other injury.[7]

When using the urgency exception to competition, an agency may limit competition to the firms it reasonably believes can perform the work in the time available. However, an agency is not permitted to award a noncompetitive contract where the urgent need has been brought about due to a lack of advanced planning. Unlike the other exceptions to competition provided by the FAR, awards that use the urgency exception have certain time restrictions. Specifically, the total period of performance is limited to the time necessary to meet the requirement and for the agency to enter into another contract through the use of competitive procedures. Further, the period of performance may not exceed 1 year unless the head of the agency or appointed designee determines that exceptional circumstances apply.

Justification for Other Than Full and Open Competition

When preparing a justification for other than full and open competition, agencies are required to include the following information:

- Identification of the agency and the contracting activity, and specific identification of the document as a "justification for other than full and open competition".
- Nature and/or description of the action being approved.
- Description of the supplies and services required to meet the agency's needs, including the estimated value.
- Identification of the statutory authority permitting other than full and open competition.
- Demonstration that the proposed contractor's unique qualifications or the nature of the acquisition requires use of the authority cited.
- Description of efforts made to ensure that offers are solicited from as many potential sources as is practicable, including whether a notice was or will be publicized.
- Determination by the contracting officer that the anticipated cost to the government will be fair and reasonable.
- Description of the market research conducted and the results of the research or a statement as to why market research was not conducted.
- Any other facts supporting use of other than full and open competition, such as an explanation why technical data packages, engineering descriptions, statements of work suitable for full and open competition have not been developed or are not available. When the urgency exception is cited, data, estimated cost, or other rationale as to the extent and nature of the harm to the Government.
- A listing of the sources, if any, that expressed, in writing, an interest in the acquisition.
- Statement of the actions, if any, the agency may take to remove or overcome any barriers to competition before subsequent acquisitions for the supplies or services are required.
- Contracting officer certification that the justification is accurate and complete to the best of the officer's knowledge and belief.

Source: Federal Acquisition Regulation.

Figure 1. Elements of a Justification for Other Than Full and Open Competition Required by the FAR.

Generally, noncompetitive awards must be supported by written justifications that contain sufficient facts and rationale to justify use of the specific exception to competition that is being applied to the procurement. At a minimum, justifications must include 12 elements specified in the FAR, including a description of the goods and services being procured, market research conducted, and efforts to solicit offers, among other things, as shown in figure 1.

For noncompetitive awards using the urgency exception, justifications may be prepared and approved within a reasonable time after award when doing so prior to award would unreasonably delay the acquisition. Justifications are to be published—on the Federal Business Opportunities website (FedBizOpps)—generally, within 30 days after contract award.[8] Additionally, justifications must be approved at various levels within the contracting organization. These levels vary according to the estimated total dollar value of the proposed contract, including all options. As outlined in table 1, the approval levels range from the contracting officer for smaller dollar contracts up to the agency's senior procurement executive for larger dollar contracts.

Table 1. FAR Approval Levels for Justifications for Other Than Full and Open Competition

Estimated value of proposed contract action	Approval by
$650,000 or less	Contracting officer
Over $650,000 but not exceeding $12.5 million	Competition advocate for the procuring activity or officials authorized to approve at a higher level
Over $12.5 million but not exceeding $62.5 million ($85.5 million for DOD, NASA[a], and Coast Guard)	Head of the procuring activity, or designee meetingcertain criteria
More than $62.5 million (or $85.5 million for DOD, NASA, and Coast Guard)	Agency senior procurement executive

Source: Federal Acquisition Regulation.

[a]National Aeronautics and Space Administration

The FAR has more streamlined procedures for awarding contracts under the simplified acquisition threshold—generally less than $150,000. These smaller dollar awards are exempt from the justification and documentation requirements described above for contracts over this threshold. For example, contracting officers awarding a contract under simplified acquisition procedures must only document the determination that competition was not feasible; no approval beyond the contracting officer is required. Further, agencies do not have to document the extent and nature of the harm to the government that necessitates limiting competition when using simplified acquisition procedures. When using these procedures, agencies may solicit an offer from one contractor in certain circumstances, including when the contracting officer determines that only one source is reasonably available.[9]

In general, once a contract is awarded, the awarding agency must enter certain information into FPDS-NG, the federal government's database that captures information on contract awards and obligations. Agencies are responsible for the quality of the information entered into the database. Data captured includes, for example, the contract value, whether the contract was awarded competitively or not, and what authority was used to award the contract noncompetitively. In FPDS-NG, there are three fields for agencies to report competition data for contracts awarded:

- Extent competed: the competitive nature of the contract awarded, for example, whether the contract was awarded using full and open competition or not competed using simplified acquisition procedures.
- Solicitation procedure: the procedure an agency used to solicit offers for a proposed contract opportunity, for example, soliciting an offer from only one contractor because the agency deemed only one source available to fulfill the need or soliciting offers pursuant to simplified acquisition procedures.
- Other than full and open competition: the reason an award was not competed and the authority used to forego full and open competition, for example, the unusual and compelling urgency exception to competition. For the purposes of this report, we refer to this field as "the reason not competed" to be more descriptive of the content in the field.

AGENCIES USED THE URGENCY EXCEPTION TO A LIMITED EXTENT AND PROCURED A RANGE OF GOODS AND SERVICES, BUT DATA RELIABILITY IS QUESTIONABLE

DOD's, State's, and USAID's Use of the Urgency Exception Is Small Compared to Other Exceptions to Competition

Based on data from FPDS-NG, DOD, State, and USAID obligations for contracts and task orders reported as using the urgency exception during fiscal years 2010 through 2012 were small relative to other exceptions to full and open competition.[10] Of the $998 billion that DOD obligated for all contracts during this period, $432 billion or 43 percent were awarded noncompetitively; however, only about $12.5 billion—or about 3 percent— of DOD's noncompetitive obligations were awarded under the urgency exception. Less than 1 percent of USAID's noncompetitive obligations— $3.3 billion—were obligated under the urgency exception. In comparison to DOD and USAID, State's obligations under the urgency exception were more substantial, accounting for 12.5 percent—or $582 million—of its noncompetitive obligations, as shown in figure 2.

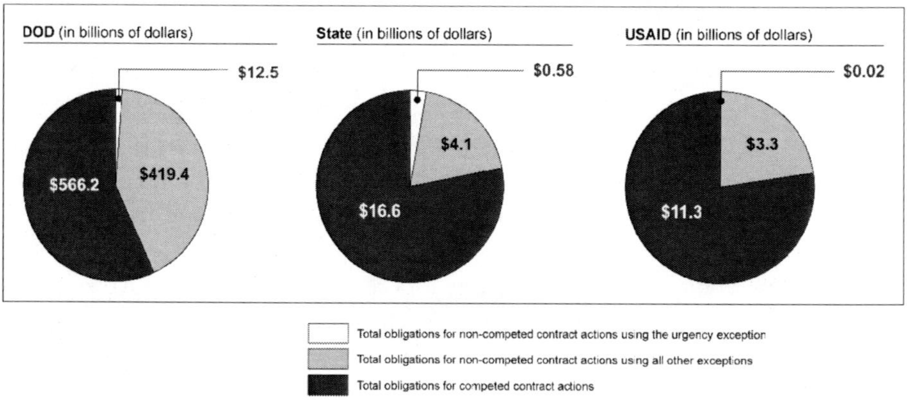

Source: GAO analysis of federal procurement data.

Figure 2. Percent of Total Competitive and Noncompetitive Obligations for DOD, State, and USAID, Including Use of the Urgency Exception Compared to Use of Other Exceptions to Competition, Fiscal Years 2010 through 2012.

DOD's obligations under the urgency exception accounted for more than 85 percent of the total dollars obligated using the urgency exception across the federal government from fiscal years 2010 through 2012. Among civilian agencies, State and USAID obligations using the urgency exception accounted for about 4 percent and less than 1 percent of total urgency obligations across the federal government, respectively. DOD and USAID's obligations under the urgency exception remained relatively constant for fiscal years 2010 through 2012; however, State's obligations in fiscal year 2011 were $301.4 million, more than a twelvefold increase over its fiscal year 2010 obligations, which totaled $24.4 million. Most of the increase can be attributed to three contracts, which altogether totaled more than 75 percent of State's total urgency obligations in fiscal year 2011.[11]

Agencies Procured a Range of Goods and Services Using the Urgency Exception

Our analysis of FPDS-NG data showed that use of the urgency exception varied in the types of goods and services acquired across DOD, State, and USAID for fiscal years 2010 through 2012. As figure 3 shows, State and USAID obligated funds to almost exclusively procure services while DOD obligated funds to procure an equal percentage of goods and services. During the 3-year period, DOD procured a broad range of items with more than half of funds—or over $6 billion—for research and development and to purchase communications and radar equipment. For State, about 60 percent of funds—over $335 million—were obligated to procure guard protection services at U.S. embassies and other facilities. For USAID, nearly half of its funds—more than $9 million—were obligated to support construction of roads and highways and to procure education and training services.

Coding Errors and Limitations Highlight Federal Procurement Data Reliability Concerns

We found coding errors in FPDS-NG for contracts awarded by DOD, State, and USAID. Specifically, of the 62 contracts we selected for our sample, 28 were reported in FPDS-NG as being awarded noncompetitively using the urgency exception, but were not. Of the 28 contracts that were not correctly reported in FPDS-NG, three contracts were awarded using other exceptions to competition, such as national security, five were awarded using a unique authority to award noncompetitive contracts at USAID, and 20 contracts were awarded using simplified acquisition procedures. We note that our sample is not representative of all dollars obligated for federal contracts.

We found three Air Force contracts that were incorrectly coded in FPDS-NG as awarded using the urgency exception to competition, but the contract file documentation confirmed that these contracts were awarded noncompetitively on the basis of national security concerns or that only one vendor could supply the requirement. Of these three contracts, two were awarded noncompetitively to procure an unmanned aircraft system and replacement aircraft accessories on the basis that disclosure of the agency's need would compromise national security. Officials explained that these coding errors were due to an administrative oversight. For the remaining contract which was awarded on the basis that only one contractor could perform the work, officials identified and corrected the error during a routine inspection that occurred after we included the contract in our sample.

Agency	Percentage of goods and services procured	Examples of goods procured	Examples of services procured
DOD	$6 billion; $6.5 billion	Goods procured included weapons, ammunition, and explosives; aircraft and vehicle components; radar equipment; personal armor; and clothing to protect against improvised explosive devices; and medical equipment and supplies.	Services procured included research and development of systems; engineering and technical support; information technology and telecommunications; equipment maintenance; program management and administrative support; education and training,operating air traffic towers, sewage and waste treatment and storage, and garbage collection.
State	$30.1 million; $550.8 million	Goods procured included radio and television equipment, prefabricated doors and windows, and generators.	Services were procured to provide security, internet and telecommunications; and administrative and management support. In addition, other procurements categorized as services included travel and lodging, and facilities support to operate government-occupied buildings such as the U.S. embassy in Iraq.
USAID	$0.07 million; $19.4 million	All goods procured for this time period were reported in the federal procurement database as miscellaneous items, which are defined as items which cannot be otherwise classified in any existing federal procurement database class.	Services that were procured included education and training; engineering and program management support, contractors to perform personal services, such as providing short-term transition assistance in conflict prone countries; and construction of roads, bridges, and railways.

Goods
Services

Source: GAO analysis of federal procurement data.

Figure 3. Percentage of DOD, State, and USAID Dollars Obligated for Goods and Services and Examples of Items Procured Using the Urgency Exception for Fiscal Years 2010 through 2012.

We identified five USAID contracts that were noncompetitive awards using an authority unique to USAID that allows the agency to award noncompetitive contracts where competition would impair or otherwise have an adverse effect on programs conducted for the purposes of foreign aid, relief, and rehabilitation.[12] FPDS-NG does not include an option to report noncompetitive awards using USAID's unique exception to competition. Thus, according to USAID officials, contracting staff use their professional judgment to choose an option in FPDS-NG that most closely matches the circumstances of the award. This may include reporting the noncompeted award as being procured using the urgency exception. We did not assess the extent to which USAID consistently reported these awards using the urgency exception versus other exceptions to competition.

Twenty of the contracts were awarded for less than $150,000 using simplified acquisition procedures. These contracts were awarded noncompetitively on the basis that the good or service was required immediately and only one source was deemed reasonably available. The contract file documentation showed that DOD, State, and USAID procured various goods and services—including water purification systems, furniture storage space, drapes and holiday gifts—using streamlined procedures for simplified acquisitions. However, when recording the reason these contracts were not competed in FPDS-NG, DOD, State, and USAID incorrectly reported that these contracts were awarded using the unusual and compelling urgency exception to full and open competition. Contracting officials attributed these coding errors to an administrative oversight and some officials admitted to confusion about how to input data in FPDS-NG. Such inaccurate reporting adds to existing concerns about the reliability of some data elements in FPDS-NG which GAO has reported on previously.[13]

For the 20 contracts awarded using simplified procedures, we found that the potential for confusion arises when agencies are directed in FPDSNG to record the solicitation procedure and the extent to which a contract was competed. Based on our analysis of contracts reported as using the urgency exception to competition, when reporting which solicitation procedure was used, contracting staff frequently selected the entry labeled "only one source." This denotes that the agency did not solicit offers from potential vendors because it determined only one source was reasonably available given the urgent need. Agencies also selected the entry labeled "not competed" when reporting the extent to which a contract was competed.

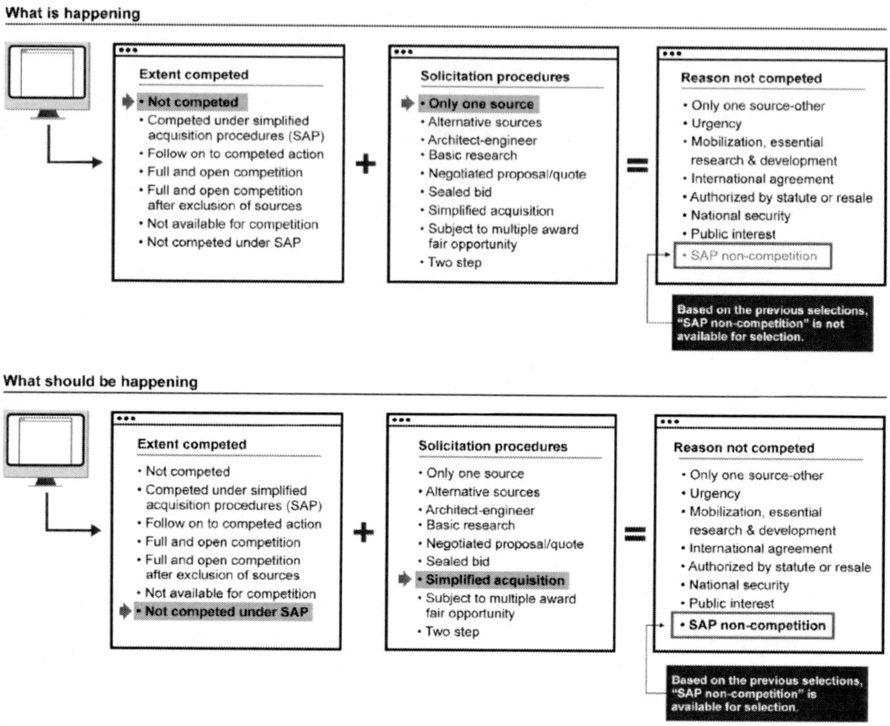

Source: GAO analysis of Federal Procurement Data System-Next Generation documents.

Figure 4. Illustration of Data Entry Practices and FPDS-NG Validation Rules for Contracts Awarded Using Simplified Procedures.

As figure 4 illustrates, when contracting staff select "only one source" in the solicitation procedure field, FPDS-NG validation rules do not allow the selection of simplified acquisition procedures in the field for the "reason not competed". For these contracts, per FPDS-NG instructions, contracting staff should have reported these awards as "simplified acquisition" under solicitation procedure and "not competed under simplified acquisition procedures" in the extent competed field. Consistent with FPDS-NG database instructions, using this approach would restrict the data entry options available when reporting the reason not competed to simplified acquisition procedures. During the course of our review, the Defense Logistics Agency (DLA) within DOD used this approach to correct the entry in FPDS-NG for two awards under $150,000 that are now recorded as sole-source awards using simplified acquisition procedures which is consistent with the records maintained in the corresponding contract files. In 2010, DOD issued guidance to, among other things, help improve the quality of data reported in FPDS-NG for contracts awarded using simplified acquisition procedures. For fiscal years 2010 through 2012, data in FPDS-NG showed that collectively DOD, State, and USAID reported 13,040 noncompetitive contracts under $150,000 as being awarded under the urgency exception. The total obligation for these contracts was over $284 million. Ensuring contracts are correctly coded in FPDS-NG is critical as the data are used to inform procurement policy decisions and facilitate congressional oversight.

Agencies Cited a Range of Urgent Circumstances to Award Noncompetitive Contracts and Justifications Generally Contained Required Elements

After excluding the contracts we identified with data errors, we found that 34 contracts were awarded noncompetitively using the unusual and compelling urgency exception to competition to meet a range of urgent situations.[14] Our sample included DOD contracts that were awarded to meet urgent operational needs for combat operations in Afghanistan and Iraq, including two contracts that highlight the risk of using the urgency exception for research and development initiatives to immediately field capabilities for combat operations. In addition, our sample consisted of contracts awarded to avoid a lapse in program support resulting from firms protesting the award of a competitive contract or from changes in program requirements. Generally, noncompetitive awards—such as those using the urgency exception—must be supported by written justifications that contain the facts and rationale to justify use of an exception to competition. While justifications in our sample generally contained the required information, some fell short of the FAR requirements and did not obtain the necessary signatures or make justifications publicly available. Other justifications were written ambiguously in terms of including other facts supporting the use of the urgency exception, such as the nature of the harm to the government.

Agencies Awarded Noncompetitive Contracts to Meet a Range of Urgent Situations

For the 34 contracts in our sample, DOD, State, and USAID cited a range of urgent situations that precluded full and open competition. More than half of the contracts were awarded to procure goods and services to support various missions in Afghanistan and Iraq. The two most common reasons agencies cited for awarding noncompetitive contracts on the basis of urgency—sometimes for the same contract—were to meet urgent operational needs for combat operations and to avoid a gap in program support resulting from unanticipated events. The remaining contracts supported unique circumstances such as fulfilling increased demand for fuel, providing telecommunications support for a foreign delegation visit, obtaining equipment for an unscheduled naval mission, and addressing emergency vehicle repairs. See Appendix II for a summary of the 34 contracts in our sample.

DOD Sought to Meet Urgent Operational Needs for Combat Operations

DOD awarded 16 contracts, valued at $1.2 billion, to rapidly acquire and provide capabilities to meet urgent needs that, DOD maintained, if not addressed immediately, would seriously endanger personnel or pose a threat to ongoing combat operations. These needs involved two primary capabilities: intelligence, surveillance, and reconnaissance (ISR)—such as airships—and systems to protect against attacks from improvised explosive devices. DOD's acquisition policy states that urgent operational needs are among the highest priority acquisitions and identifies the urgency exception as one of the tools available to provide urgently needed capabilities to the warfighter more quickly by reducing the amount of time needed to award a contract.[15] In an April 2012 report, GAO found that some DOD programs to meet urgent operational needs were able to reach contract award sooner by relying on urgent noncompetitive awards; however, this reliance could affect the price the government pays.[16]

Recognizing the need to quickly deliver capabilities in urgent conditions — sometimes within days or months—DOD policy calls for delivering solutions for urgent needs within 24 months of when the urgent operational need is identified and validated. Within the sample of urgent DOD awards we reviewed, many of the capabilities acquired in response to urgent operational needs were fielded within 3 to 20 months of when the requirement was identified. For example, by relying on an existing technology, the Army was able to quickly field 29 surveillance aerostats within 10 months of validating the urgent operational need. DOD contracting officials we spoke with told us they expect decreases in the number of noncompetitive awards on the basis of urgency to meet urgent operational needs because of the drawdown in military operations in Iraq and Afghanistan.

Two DOD awards within our sample highlighted the risks of using the urgency exception to competition to award contracts for research and development initiatives to meet immediate combat operation needs. DOD policy identifies efforts best suited for rapid fielding of urgently needed capabilities as those that do not require substantial development effort, are based on proven and available technologies, and can be acquired under a fixed price contract.

In the first example, the Air Force's Blue Devil Block 2 program used the urgency exception to purchase previously unproven technology for improved ISR capability. GAO and the DOD Inspector General have previously reported that the program faced various challenges.[17] In 2009, the Air Force first identified the need for the program following a presentation from the contractor for an airship concept that could take off and land vertically while requiring fewer personnel to assist with landing than traditional airships. In March 2010, the contractor submitted an unsolicited proposal to the Air Force for the development of the Blue Devil Block 2 airship. The Air Force Research Laboratory (AFRL) conducted an assessment of the program and determined that the proposed 24 month schedule was aggressive and likely unachievable. As an alternative, AFRL proposed a strategy to develop the airship in 34 months using competitive procedures. In September 2010, the Secretary of Defense designated the procurement of the airship as an urgent need to be rapidly acquired, and set the expectation that it be deployed within 13 months. The following month, AFRL conducted a second assessment of the program and again determined that it was not suitable for rapid fielding within 24 months due to concerns about the technical capability of the contractor and poorly defined requirements. Despite AFRL's assessment, the Air Force awarded an $86.2 million contract in March 2011 based on urgency for delivery of the airship in January 2012. In an October 2012 report, GAO found that this program experienced significant technical problems resulting in cost overruns and schedule delays that led to termination of the program in June 2012, which was 5 months after the planned fielding date of January 2012.[18] Ultimately, the program was terminated after spending more than $149 million and without fulfilling the urgent requirement for a deployable ISR airship.

In the second example, the Air Force awarded a noncompetitive contract in 2011 on the basis of urgency for the development of the Orion unmanned aerial system in response to an urgent operational need for ISR capabilities to support multiple services in Afghanistan. The new system was expected to provide greater uninterrupted flight times than other available systems. The contract was awarded with a period of performance of 13 months; however, the justification did not specify a fielding date. After award, the cost of the contract nearly tripled from the initial estimate of $5 million to a total of about $15 million and the period of performance doubled from 13 months to 26 months. Contracting officials said that cost increases and schedule delays were due to technical problems experienced by the contractor in developing the proposed technology. Nearly 3 years since the requirement was validated as an urgent need, this system has not been fielded in Afghanistan and is still under development through a follow-on contract.

GAO has previously found that initiatives for urgent operational needs that required technology development often take longer to field.[19] Contracting officials we spoke with said that both programs relied heavily on unproven technologies that required extensive research and development, which contributed, in part, to the cancelation and delay of the Blue Devil and Orion systems, respectively. Further, officials noted that initiatives to respond to urgent operational needs tend to have more successful outcomes when the solutions are based on proven, mature technologies.

Agencies Sought to Avoid a Gap in Program Support Resulting from Unanticipated Events

DOD, State, and USAID awarded 12 noncompetitive contracts when unexpected events threatened the agencies' ability to continue program support. Referred to as bridge contracts, such awards are typically short term to avoid a lapse in program support while the award of a follow-on contract is being planned. The contract period for the 12 bridge awards in our sample averaged 11 months and collectively they were valued at a total of over $466 million. For the bridge contracts that we reviewed, the delay in awarding a competitive contract was due to unforeseen personnel changes, competitors filing bid protests, and changes in program requirements, among other things. For 10 of the 12 bridge contracts in our sample, agencies awarded the contract to a vendor that had previously performed the work.

- In one instance, the Air Force's plans to competitively award a follow-on contract for engineering support services was disrupted by the unexpected loss of the program manager who had specialized expertise and had been working independently on the acquisition strategy for about 1 year. A new program manager was assigned but had difficulty accessing his predecessor's files which further delayed the acquisition effort. The justification cited that a gap in program support would jeopardize ongoing research and expose the Air Force to certain fines and penalties. Faced with the possibility of costly delays estimated to be $1.5 million per month, the Air Force opted to award a non-competitive bridge contract to the incumbent vendor who was deemed most capable of meeting the program's requirements within the timeframes needed. Officials determined that the 12-month bridge contract valued at $1.4 million would provide sufficient time to complete market research and other acquisition planning for the subsequent award.

- In another instance, State awarded a competitive follow-on contract to provide operational and maintenance support services at the U.S. Embassy compound in Baghdad, Iraq, three months before the existing contract expired. However, the new contract, which was awarded to the incumbent vendor, was protested, thus preventing the contractor from starting performance on the contract. Citing concerns about the health and safety of 4,200 U.S. government personnel, State awarded a 6-month bridge contract valued at $38 million to the incumbent vendor to ensure continuity of services. The justification cited that transitioning to a contractor other than the incumbent vendor would take at least 90 days because of visa processing, among other things.
- A USAID program for oversight, outreach, and legislative assistance to the National Assembly of Afghanistan was extended to ensure continued support to the Afghan parliament during the upcoming budget cycle. The contract USAID planned to use to obtain these services was not awarded in time. As a result, USAID awarded a 7-month bridge contract to the incumbent vendor with a value of $5 million to avoid a break in service, with the goal of awarding a competitive follow-on contract during the parliament's upcoming summer recess. USAID determined that for the bridge contract, a new vendor could not transition within the time available due to security clearances and other requirements.

Justifications Generally Contained the Required Elements and Provided Varied Levels of Insight about the Risks that Led to Use of the Urgency Exception

Justifications in our sample generally contained the required information; however, some fell short of the FAR requirements and did not obtain the necessary signatures, among other things. Other justifications were written ambiguously in terms of including other facts supporting the use of the urgency exception, such as the nature of the harm to the government.

Justifications Generally Contained the Required Elements, Yet Several Did Not Meet All FAR Requirements

Consistent with acquisition regulations, DOD, State, and USAID prepared written justifications for all of the 34 urgent contracts in our sample to include the required elements specified in the FAR—such as the contracting officer's determination that the cost will be fair and reasonable and the extent of the agencies' market research efforts. In addition, nearly all of the justifications that we reviewed were prepared and approved prior to award. The FAR permits agencies to prepare and approve justifications within a reasonable time after contract award when doing so prior to award would unreasonably delay the acquisition. This provision is unique to use of the urgency exception, as preparation and approval of the justification prior to award can delay the quick response time needed to meet urgent needs. Contracting officials told us that they work together with the program office to prepare justifications and, at a minimum, obtain verbal approvals when it is unlikely the justification can be routed to approving officials prior to award.

In three instances, however, we found justifications were not signed by the appropriate approving authority as required by the FAR. For example, a USAID justification to award a $5 million contract to support missions in Afghanistan was not signed by the Competition Advocate due to an administrative oversight. In a second example, officials at the Defense Logistics Agency did not obtain the necessary written approvals justifying a $32 million award for an emergency fuel purchase also due to an administrative oversight; however, according to officials, verbal approvals had been obtained from all requisite approving officials including the head of the contracting activity prior to award. After we brought this to their attention, DLA officials obtained the necessary signatures on the justification for this contract, even though the contract was complete. The office that awarded this contract has since put a tool in place to route justifications and ensure appropriate signatures are obtained in a timely manner. Lastly, an Air Force justification for a noncompetitive award valued at $130 million was not signed by the Senior Procurement Executive, as required by the FAR. Officials we spoke with could not confirm the reason the procurement executive did not sign the justification and this individual is no longer employed by the Air Force.

We also found four DOD justifications that were not signed in time to meet the FAR requirement to make them publicly available within 30 days of award. While the FAR permits agencies to prepare and approve justifications awarded using the urgency exception within a reasonable time after award; it does not identify a specific timeframe to do so. However, agencies are required to make justifications for urgent noncompetitive contracts available on the FedBizOpps website within 30 days of award.[20] Thus, agencies would need to prepare and approve justifications within 30 days in order to meet FAR requirements to make them publicly available. DOD contracting officials who administered the awards included in our sample told us it is customary to obtain verbal approvals on justifications for noncompetitive procurements prior to award; but such justifications are not made publicly available without signatures from the appropriate approving official. The justifications for these contracts were not signed until 58 to 314 days after award, meaning that the fully approved justifications were not made publicly available within 30 days of award as required by the FAR. In one of these cases, an Army justification for a 3-month noncompetitive award for satellite equipment was not prepared and approved, in writing, until 138 days after award. Citing concerns about compliance, the Army attorney who provided legal review of the justification noted the absence of regulatory procedure or agency policy when approval of the justification has far exceeded the timing requirements for making the justification publicly available. Officials subsequently posted the justification which occurred more than 6 months after the contract award date and 90 days after the contract expired. Some DOD, State, and USAID contracting officials we spoke with emphasized the importance of complying with the posting requirement to provide transparency into agency's contracting activity, but others were unsure of the appropriate course of action when approval of the justification does not occur within 30 days.

For 15 of the justifications we reviewed, we could not confirm whether justifications were posted to the FedBizOpps website within the required timeframes, or at all, as no documentation was available. The FAR does not require agencies to maintain documentation that the justification was made publicly available; however, we found that in some instances, officials printed the confirmation page from the FedBizOpps website to document compliance with the requirement. After we brought this issue to their attention, officials subsequently posted five justifications. Some officials told us that justifications were not posted due to an administrative oversight.

DOD, State, and USAID have developed guidance to implement FAR requirements for justifications for noncompetitive contracts; however, none of the agencies have included instructions addressing how staff should document compliance with the FAR requirement to make justifications publicly available or what to do when the justification is not approved and ready for posting within 30 days. USAID officials acknowledged the benefit of documenting that the justification was posted to demonstrate the posting requirement was met and told us they would include a process to do so in their guidance to contracting officers. *Standards for Internal Control in the Federal Government* states that internal controls—such as agency policies and procedures—are an integral part of an organization's management function that provides reasonable assurance of compliance with laws and regulations. Control activities include the creation and maintenance of records which provide evidence of implementation, such as documentation of transactions that is readily available for inspection.[21] Contracting officials told us that documenting their efforts to make the justification publicly available provides transparency into the steps they took to comply with applicable regulations.

Justifications Provided Varied Levels of Insight about Risks

Generally, justifications for the 34 contracts in our sample described the nature of the harm—serious financial or other risk—facing the government if the award were to be delayed using traditional competitive procedures. Some justifications were specific about the potential harm to the government while others were ambiguous. The FAR states that agencies may use the urgency exception when delay of the contract award would pose a serious injury—financial or other—to the government. The FAR further provides that agencies are to include other facts, such as data, estimated cost, or other rationale as to the extent and nature of the harm to the government —which provides some flexibility about how such risks should be described in the justification.

Most of the justifications in our sample—23 of 34—quantified the potential harm to the government if the acquisition was delayed by using competitive procedures in terms of potential dollars lost or schedule delays. The Air Force and the Army have guidance for preparing justifications which states that the most critical aspect of justifications that cite use of the urgency exception is quantifying the nature of the serious injury to the government if the urgent requirement is competed.[22] Accordingly, nearly all of the Air Force and Army justifications we reviewed estimated the potential costs to the government if the urgent award were to be delayed by using competitive procedures. For instance, one Air Force justification for an unmanned aerial system explained that no other vendors had mature technology and estimated that the effort of bringing at least one other vendor to an equivalent capability would cost $5.7 million and result in at least a 3-month delay. Further, the justification stated that it is unlikely these costs would be recovered through competition. Similarly, the justification for an Army contract to obtain new parts for tactical wheeled vehicles to help protect against attacks from improvised explosive devices estimated that DOD would incur $2.5 million in transportation costs if the parts were not acquired by a certain date to meet the time frame of a scheduled ship deployment.

By contrast, 11 of the justifications we reviewed were more ambiguous in describing the nature of the harm if a noncompetitive contract was not awarded. Some of the ambiguous justifications described the following:

- At Navy, justifications for four procurements to provide goods or services related to persistent ground surveillance systems cited that only one source was available as other sources would duplicate costs or cause delays. The justifications did not provide additional information about the potential time or dollars to be saved by using the urgency exception.
- At State, one justification cited the need to award a noncompetitive contract using the urgency exception to provide telecommunications support for a meeting of foreign leaders. The justification emphasized the vendor's prior experience in providing similar services, thereby facilitating the agency's mission in the most cost-effective manner. But it did not provide additional information regarding the extent and nature of the harm posed to the government. For such events, according to agency officials, security concerns often hinder the agency's ability to conduct advanced planning; thus necessitating the use of the urgency exception.
- Two USAID justifications did not fully describe the harm to the government. The justifications cited the need to comply with a requirement to conduct annual financial audits of local expenses incurred in Afghanistan; however, the extent and nature of the serious risk of financial or other injury to the government was not stated. Officials justified the noncompetitive award citing a shortage of

qualified audit firms in Afghanistan which could affect USAID's ability to meet auditing requirements. Thus, awarding a noncompetitive contract would provide an opportunity to assess the audit capabilities of the selected contractor, develop a pool of acceptable audit firms to choose from thereby increasing competition for future procurements.

AGENCIES DID NOT ALWAYS LIMIT THE DURATION TO 1 YEAR AND ACHIEVED LIMITED COMPETITION IN SELECTED INSTANCES

The FAR limits the total period of performance of contracts awarded using the urgency exception to 1 year—unless a determination from the head of the agency is made that exceptional circumstances apply. This provides the time necessary to enter into another contract using competitive procedures, which reduces the risk of overspending. Within our sample of 34 contracts, nearly a third of the contracts—10—had a period of performance that was more than 1 year, either established at the time of award or during performance of the contract. Two of these contracts exceeded 1 year at award and the contracting officers did not obtain a determination from the head of the agency, as required by the FAR. The remaining eight contracts were extended beyond 1 year through subsequent modifications, which contracting officials considered separate contract actions that, in their view, would not require a determination by the head of the agency. Treating modifications to contracts awarded on the basis of urgency as separate rather than cumulative contract actions makes it harder for senior department officials to provide oversight over significant increases in contract cost. DOD, State, and USAID conducted limited competitions for 4 of the 34 contracts in our sample by using knowledge from recent competitions to solicit multiple bids. Lack of technical data rights and reliance on the expertise of the contractor limited the agencies' abilities to seek competition.

Approaches Used to Extend Period of Performance Beyond 1 Year and to Increase Funding Diminish Oversight

We found that 10 of the 34 contracts in our sample had either a period of performance of more than 1 year at the time of award or, the period of performance was extended beyond 1 year during performance of the contract. The FAR provides that the contract period should be limited to the time required to meet the urgent need and for the agency to compete and award another contract for the required goods and services. In addition, contracts may not exceed more than 1 year unless the head of agency, or their designee, determines that exceptional circumstances apply. Limiting the length of noncompetitive awards under the urgency exception helps minimize the risk of overspending while providing sufficient time for the agency to enter into another contract using competitive procedures, according to officials from the OFPP—the office within OMB which provides governmentwide guidance on federal contracting.

In 2 of the 10 cases, we found that DOD officials did not seek a determination from the head of the agency or appropriate designee, as required, for awards where it was known at time of award that the period of performance would be more than 1 year. In one of these instances at the Navy, the justification estimated a 9-month contract period; however, the award documents indicate a total period of performance of 17 months that included 5 months for delivery of upgraded radio kits to protect against attacks from improvised explosive devices followed by 12 months of engineering support services.[23] Navy officials acknowledged that the period of performance at time of award was ambiguous and said they did not seek a determination because the terms and conditions of the contract had not yet been finalized at the time work began. In the other case at the Air Force, work on the contract began under a pre-contract cost agreement prior to the contract award date and the contract identifies the period of performance as beginning on the date the pre-contract cost agreement started. As a result, the period of performance at award was 13 months. Air Force officials told us they did not get the determination because the contract was expected to end within 12 months of the award date and they did not consider the pre-contract cost agreement as part of the period of performance for the contract, contrary to the language in the contract.

In the remaining eight instances, we found that DOD, State, and USAID used different approaches to modify the contracts to extend the period of performance beyond 1 year after the initial contract award. While the FAR clearly limits the period of performance to 1 year, it does not address whether the duration requirement applies only at the time of award or if the requirement applies to cases where the contract is modified to extend the period of performance after award. Contracting officials did not seek a determination of exceptional circumstances from the head of the agency or appropriate designee before extending the period of performance beyond 1 year. In four of the eight instances, officials extended the period of performance through contract modifications and no additional action was taken. For the remaining four instances, officials exercised a contract clause to extend the contract or prepared an additional justification to extend the contract beyond 1 year.[24]

Using a Contract Clause to Extend the Contract for 6 Months

In two of the eight cases, contracting officials extended the contracts beyond 1 year by using a contract clause that allows agencies to extend services up to 6 months within the limits and at the rates specified in the contract.[25] For urgent, noncompetitive contracts where the 1 year duration requirement applies, the FAR is not clear about whether a determination of exceptional circumstances is necessary when using this clause results in the contract's period of performance exceeding a year. In one of the two cases, for example, State awarded a 1-year bridge contract (4 month base contract with two 4 month options) to the incumbent vendor—with an estimated value of $100 million—using the urgency exception to procure local guard services in Afghanistan. The bridge contract was intended to allow time for a new contractor—the awardee of a competitive award—to set up its operations to take over the performance of these services. However, during the bridge contract period of performance, State realized that the new awardee could not establish its operations to meet the timeframes required in the contract and therefore defaulted, leading to termination of the competitive award. To allow sufficient time to re-compete the requirement and transition to a new vendor, State used the contract clause to extend the existing bridge contract for an additional 6 months but did not seek a determination of exceptional circumstances. The additional time increased the total period of performance to 18 months and added $78 million to the contract value—which included retention bonuses to provide an incentive for guards to continue working in the event the contract was extended beyond 1 year. The contracting officer did not take into consideration whether using this clause would have any bearing on the requirement to seek a determination of exceptional circumstances for an urgency award exceeding 1 year. Contracting officials we spoke with maintained that an additional determination was not required because the terms of the contract included the clause to extend services. As a result, no additional oversight occurred when the contract's period of performance exceeded 1 year.

Preparing an Additional Justification

In two of the eight cases, we found that contracting officials extended the period of performance beyond a year after award through the preparation of additional justifications for other than full and open competition. Contracting officials at DOD, State, and USAID stated their belief that urgency contracts could be extended without a determination of exceptional circumstances by the head of agency when using this approach. In their view, each additional justification represents an individual contract action; thus, there is no need to consider the cumulative effect of a modification resulting in a period of performance beyond 1 year.[26]

In one of these instances, the Army TACOM Life Cycle Management Command identified an urgent operational need for 513 medium armored security vehicles and related support—valued at more than $757 million to support the Afghanistan National Army. To meet the timeframes for delivery, officials determined that the circumstances warranted use of a noncompetitive award on the basis of urgency to one contractor with prior experience on similar acquisitions. After identifying a multi-year requirement to provide vehicles to the Afghanistan National Army, contracting officials planned to fulfill the requirement in multiple phases. For the first phase, the Army decided to purchase 73 vehicles and prepared a noncompetitive justification citing the urgency exception for an award valued at $85.1 million—which is $0.4 million below the level that requires approval from the Senior Procurement Executive. The first phase was awarded in January 2011 as an undefinitized contract action which allows the contractor to start the work quickly without negotiating all the terms and conditions for a contract.[27] However, 3 months into the performance of the contract, another justification for a modification to the undefinitized contract action was approved by the Senior Procurement Executive using a different exception citing that only one responsible source could fulfill the procurement of the remaining 440 vehicles needed to meet the requirement. The additional justification for the second phase, valued at more than $576 million, added 3 years (a base year and two 1-year options); extending the procurement to 2014. According to the contracting officer, a determination from the head of the agency was not obtained as the second phase is considered a separate action rather than cumulative; thus the period of performance under the urgency justification would not exceed 1 year. Approving the requirement between two justifications allowed for the initial contract award to be within the 1 year period of performance as required. However, when the contract exceeded a year with the subsequent modification on the grounds that only one source was capable; no additional oversight was performed by the head of the agency to determine if exceptional circumstances applied. See appendix 3 for additional information about the 10 contracts in our sample where the period of performance was more than 1 year.

Limited Oversight of Urgent Contracts with Significant Cost Growth

In addition to extending the period of performance through the preparation of additional justifications, we found instances where agencies also increased funding on urgency contracts after award to well beyond the original contract value. For seven contracts in our sample, total obligations increased by more than 30 percent from the original estimate in the justification that was approved to award a noncompetitive contract using the urgency exception. In these cases where total obligations grew considerably, contracting officials did not alert senior procurement officials when these increases occurred. In one example, Navy officials modified a contract to provide training and other support services for a surveillance system several times which grew to more than three times the estimated value. The contract value at time of award was $30 million, and the justification was signed by the head of the procuring activity, as required by the FAR for awards greater than $12.5 million but not exceeding $85.5 million. However, after award, three modifications added a total of $31 million to the contract primarily due to cost overruns. Additionally, four modifications with accompanying justifications— because the work being added was determined to be outside the original scope of the contract—added $12 million each time, bringing the total contract value to more than $109 million, as illustrated in figure 5.

The four supplemental justifications were each approved by the competition advocate, as required. However, because each justification is contemplated individually without regard to the cumulative value of the contract, the senior procurement executive did not have an oversight mechanism to be made aware of the cost growth on this contract. If this contract had been estimated to be $109 million at the time of award, the senior procurement executive would have had oversight through approval of the justification. The FAR does not provide guidance to contracting officials on the degree of oversight senior agency officials should exercise when contract modifications significantly raise the cumulative dollar value of a contract awarded using the urgency exception.

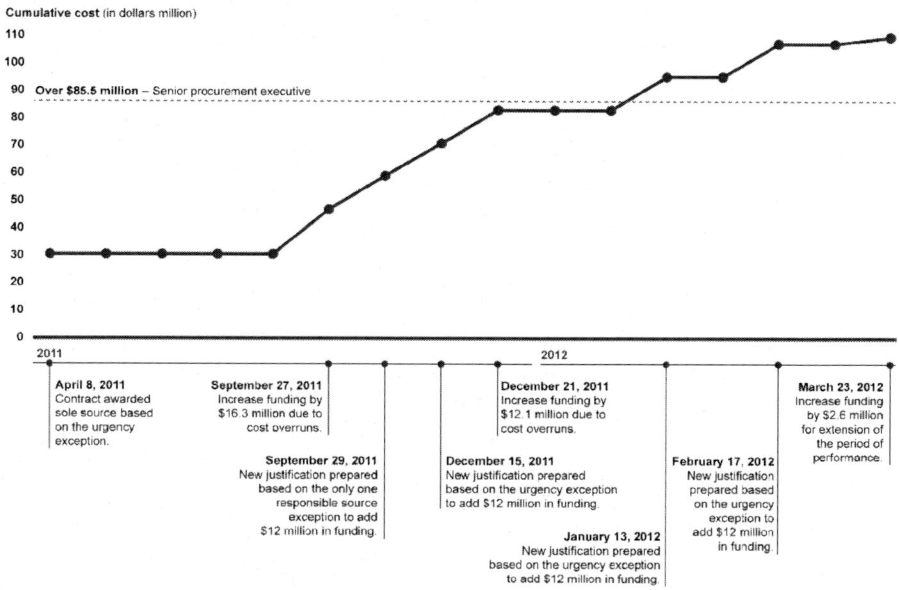

Source: GAO analysis of DOD contract documents.

Figure 5. Increases in Contract Value to Procure Training and Program Support for the Persistent Ground Surveillance System.

Using multiple modifications to increase funding or extend the period of performance and treating these as separate rather than cumulative contract actions make it harder for senior department officials to provide oversight. Competition advocates at DOD, State, and USAID had differing views about whether contract modifications to extend the period of performance should be considered cumulatively. Some thought the actions should be viewed cumulatively as it provides greater oversight; while others thought the actions should be considered independent of each other. OFPP officials told us that generally, the total period of performance of urgent contracts should be considered cumulatively either at time of award or when the contract is modified to extend the period of performance to more than 1 year. While OFPP officials stated that the period of performance should be considered cumulatively, the FAR does not specify what to do when these contracts are modified beyond 1 year, and no guidance is available on what to do in these situations. As the entity responsible for federal procurement policy, OFPP is best suited to clarify when determinations of exceptional circumstances are needed when extending the period of performance on an urgency contract beyond 1 year. Additionally, in the absence of an oversight mechanism for noncompetitive contracts awarded under the urgency exception with significant increases in value over time, senior procurement officials are not assured of the transparency necessary to help strengthen accountability for these situations. *Standards for Internal Control in the Federal Government* calls for organizations to maintain proper controls that ensure transparency and accountability for stewardship of government resources.[28]

Some Urgent Contracts Achieved Limited Competition, While Lack of Access to Technical Data Rights and Reliance on Contractor Expertise Thwarted Competition in Others

Even in urgent situations, agencies are required to seek offers from as many potential sources as practicable given the circumstances and some programs in our sample were able to use the prior expertise or market knowledge to hold limited competitions. For 4 of the 34 contracts in our sample, DOD and State sought competition by seeking offers from firms with which the agency had prior experience through recent procurements and reasonably believed could perform the work in the time available. For example, to avoid an unanticipated disruption in supplying fuel to the government of Israel, DLA solicited four firms the agency had worked with on similar acquisitions in the past. In the justification, DLA cited that having the benefit of market information from prior competitive awards helped the agency reduce the time it would normally take to compete the new procurement. In another instance, State had an existing indefinite delivery indefinite quantity contract in place for the purchase of ballistic resistant doors for embassy security. During embassy renovations it was determined that the required specification could not be met through the negotiated terms of the existing contract. State officials conducted a limited competition among three vendors who were approved vendors under the existing contract. Further, State justified this limited competition as the preferred cost-effective method as these three vendors had been the lowest bidders on similar procurements, thus, limiting the risk of overspending.

For 10 DOD contracts in our sample, the government was unable to compete requirements because of a lack of access to technical data packages or proprietary data coupled with the urgency of the requirement. In some instances, program officials explored the possibility of acquiring the data only to learn that the package was not available for sale or would be cost-prohibitive. In our prior work, DOD described the acquisition of technical data for weapon systems, such as design drawings and specifications as critical to enabling competition throughout a system's life cycle.[29] Within our sample, we found in one instance where DLA was in the process of negotiating the purchase of the technical data, but the purchase could not be completed in a timeframe that would have allowed competition for the urgent requirement. While DLA was not able to benefit from the purchase of the technical data package for the current award, the agency would be better positioned to compete future procurements. For more than a decade we have reported on the limitations to competition when DOD does not purchase technical data rights and the increased costs as a result.[30] In May 2013, DOD implemented guidance for program managers to consider acquiring technical data rights as part of the acquisition planning.

In examining the procurement history for two contracts in our sample, we found one DOD program involving an aerostat, the Persistent Threat Detection System (PTDS) that spanned 10 years without achieving competition for the acquisition of the aerostat. The Army has awarded six noncompetitive contracts for the PTDS program since 2004 on the basis of urgency to the same contractor, as illustrated in figure 6.[31]

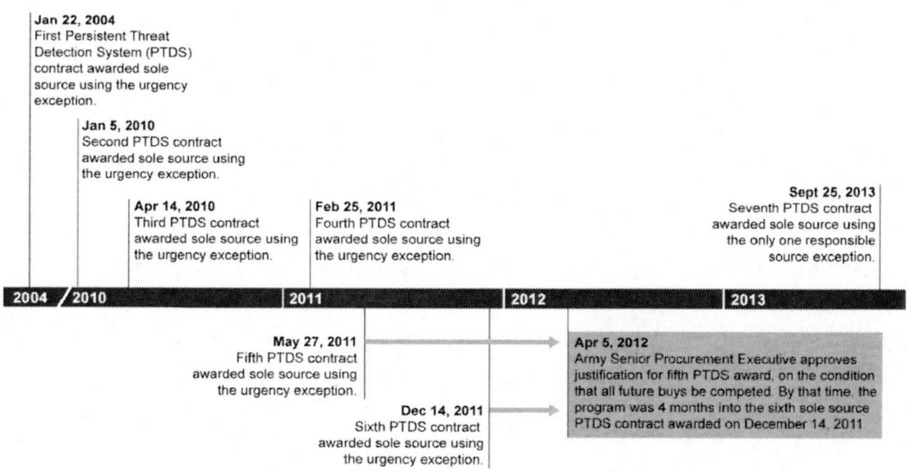

Source: GAO analysis of DOD contract documents.

Figure 6. Time Line of Events to Procure the Aerostat for the Persistent Threat Detection System Program.

While awarding the fourth PTDS contract in February 2011, the Army identified six capable sources and determined that competition was viable for long-term non-urgent requirements. However, the Army determined that only one contractor with prior experience could satisfy the urgent requirement at that time. In May 2011, the Army awarded a noncompetitive urgency contract to that contractor for 29 aerostats and cited the future need for spares in fiscal year 2012 when additional funding would be available. The senior procurement executive approved the May 2011 urgency justification nearly a year after award—due to confusion about changes in the review process—on the condition that all future related procurements be competed. However, by the time that the senior procurement executive approved the justification for the May 2011 urgent award, the Army had already awarded the follow on urgent award for spares in December 2011. While the Army identified six sources that were capable of competing and providing the PTDS aerostat in 2011, it ultimately awarded a 3-year noncompetitive contract to the same contractor valued at $306 million on the basis of "only one responsible source" because the government did not own the technical data packages. Despite the recurring nature of the requirement, Army officials reported that it was difficult to plan for competition because each requirement was short term in nature.

In 2013, DOD concurred with our recommendation to develop guidance to enable DOD components to apply lessons learned from past procurements to increase competition for the sme goods and services.[32] This recommendation was, in part, intended to help senior department officials capture the benefit of information on past procurements when approving individual justifications for subsequent noncompetitive awards. To address concerns about missed opportunities for learning why past acquisitions were not competed and to help remove barriers to competition in future procurements, in April 2013, the Air Force implemented a new policy to include justifications from predecessor acquisitions as a reference document to justification approving officials. Air Force officials observed that contracting officers were splitting requirements across multiple justifications at lower approval thresholds, which reduced oversight by higher level approving officials. The Navy has a similar policy in place and DLA officials told us they are planning to implement a similar process. The Army, which has added increased scrutiny of justifications particularly for urgency awards as one its goals for improving competition, is in the process of revising its guidance for preparing justifications to include a process similar to that of the Air Force.

CONCLUSION

The benefits of competition—such as cost savings and improved contractor performance—in acquiring goods and services from the private sector are well documented. Awarding a noncompetitive contract on the basis of unusual and compelling urgency is necessary in select circumstances. However these contracts should be limited in duration to minimize the amount of time that the government is exposed to the risks of contracts that are awarded quickly without the benefits of competition. Mechanisms for transparency and oversight of these contracts —such as posting justifications publicly and a determination that exceptional circumstance apply to extend the contract period of performance beyond 1 year—are necessary to ensuring that they are used only in circumstances when no other option is available and to promote competition in the future. Transparency and oversight during performance of the contract, particularly when adding significant time or money, ensures that the government is making sound decisions in the best interest of taxpayers. In light of this, having OFPP provide guidance to clarify when determinations are needed when extending the period of performance on an urgency contract could help achieve consistent implementation of the duration requirement across the government. Additionally, having agencies develop mechanisms to ensure that senior procurement officials are made aware of noncompetitive contracts with significant increases in value, particularly those that were not initially approved at the senior procurement executive level, could help to increase transparency in noncompetitive awards and strengthen oversight. And finally, although the data show that DOD, State, and USAID buy a relatively small amount of goods and services noncompetitively on an urgent basis, maintaining reliable data is critical to ensuring that agencies can effectively manage the use of this exception.

RECOMMENDATIONS FOR EXECUTIVE ACTION

To help improve reporting of federal procurement data and strengthen oversight of contracts awarded on the basis of an unusual and compelling urgency, we recommend the Secretaries of Defense and State and the Administrator of the U.S. Agency for International Development take the following four actions:

- Provide guidance to contracting staff on the correct procedures for accurately reporting competition data for contracts using simplified acquisition procedures that are awarded on an urgent basis and DOD should re-emphasize existing guidance.
- Establish a process for documenting that justifications were posted in compliance with the requirements in the FAR.
- Provide guidance to contracting staff on what actions to take when required signatures are not obtained in order to post the justifications within 30 days.
- Develop an oversight mechanism when the cumulative value of noncompetitive contracts awarded on the basis of unusual and compelling urgency increases considerably beyond the initial contract award value.

To help ensure consistent implementation of the FAR requirement to limit the period of performance for noncompetitive contracts using the unusual and compelling urgency exception, we recommend that the Director of the Office of Management and Budget, through the Office of Federal Procurement Policy, take the following action:

- Provide guidance to clarify when determinations of exceptional circumstances are needed when a noncompetitive contract awarded on the basis of unusual and compelling urgency exceeds 1 year, either at time of award or modified after contract award.

Agency Comments and Our Evaluation

We provided a draft of this report to DOD, State, USAID, and OMB for their review and comment. We received written comments from DOD, State and USAID. OMB provided comments via email. The agencies generally agreed with the recommendations and in most cases described planned actions in response. We also received technical comments from DOD, which we incorporated as appropriate.

DOD concurred with three recommendations and partially concurred with one recommendation. In written comments, DOD stated that the Defense Procurement and Acquisition Policy (DPAP) office will issue guidance to the contracting activities to remind them of instructions on completing data fields in FPDS-NG for simplified acquisition procedures, and to clarify documentation related to posting of justifications and actions to take when approval signatures are not obtained within the 30-day posting requirement. These actions are responsive to three of our four recommendations. For the fourth recommendation, DOD's proposed action to issue guidance emphasizing that the cumulative value of a contract should be considered when obtaining approval to increase the value of a contract awarded under the urgency exception does not fully address our recommendation. Although this guidance could be helpful, the recommendation was to develop an oversight mechanism for when contracts awarded under the urgency exception increase in value considerably over the course of time. The oversight mechanism would provide higher level contracting officials with visibility into awards that grow in small dollar increments that do not meet the thresholds for a new justification. One example of how this mechanism could be implemented would be to require approval at a higher level when the cumulative contract value increases by a certain percentage.

In written comments, State agreed with the recommendations, stating it will seek to implement them by August 30, 2014. State did not provide any further details on implementation plans.

In its written response, USAID concurred with the recommendations, and outlined steps it will take in response to them, including assessing and updating current guidance, policy and training components.

In an email response, OMB agreed that there is a need for clarification regarding the use of exceptional circumstance determinations when contracts awarded using the urgency exception exceed 1 year. These officials further noted that they intend to work with the FAR Council, which updates the FAR, to discuss the issues raised in the report about the current FAR language and the best way to address those issues.

Belva Martin
Director, Acquisition and Sourcing Management

APPENDIX I: OBJECTIVES, SCOPE, AND METHODOLOGY

The objectives for this review were to examine (1) the pattern of use of the unusual and compelling urgency exception, including the range of goods and services acquired by the Departments of Defense (DOD) and State, and US Agency for International Development's (USAID); (2) the reasons that agencies awarded noncompetitive contracts on the basis of urgency and the extent to which justifications met requirements in the Federal Acquisition Regulation (FAR); and (3) the extent to which agencies limited the duration of the contract and achieved competition.

Table 2. Contracting Offices and the Number of Contracts Reviewed

Agency	Contracting Office	Number of contracts reviewed
Air Force	Air Force Materiel Command, Hanscom Air Force Base, Massachusetts	1
	Aeronautical Systems Center, Wright Patterson Air Force Base, Ohio	5
	Air Force Research Laboratory, Wright Patterson Air Force Base, Ohio	3
Army	TACOM Life Cycle Management Command, Warren, Michigan	5
	Army Contracting Command-Aberdeen Proving Ground, Aberdeen, Maryland	6
Navy	Naval Air Systems Command, Warfare Center Aircraft Division, Lakehurst, New Jersey	5
	Naval Sea Systems Command, Washington, D.C.	5
Defense Logistics Agency (DLA)	DLA-Energy, Fort Belvoir, Virginia	3
	DLA-Land and Maritime, Warren, Michigan	4
State	Office of Acquisition Management, Arlington, Virginia	7
	American Embassy Brussels	6
USAID	Office of Acquisition and Assistance, Afghanistan	4
	Office of Acquisition and Assistance, Washington, D.C.	1
	Office of Foreign Disaster Assistance, Washington, D.C.	1
	Office of Transition Initiatives, Washington, D.C.	6

Source: GAO analysis.

To address these objectives, we used data in the Federal Procurement Data System-Next Generation (FPDS-NG), which is the government's procurement database, to identify DOD, State, and USAID obligations for noncompetitive contracts awarded using the unusual and compelling urgency exception. We selected a non-generalizable, random sample of 62 contracts by using data from FPDS-NG to analyze which components within DOD, State, and USAID had the most obligations using the urgency exception for fiscal years 2011 and 2012, which, at the time, were the most recent fiscal years for which data was available. To narrow our focus on which contracts to include in our review, we identified the contracting offices within DOD, State, and USAID that had the largest total obligations for contracts reported as being awarded using the urgency exception under the "reason not competed" field in the FPDS-NG database. We then selected contracts that represented a mix of large and smaller dollar awards and types of products and services procured. Table 2 below shows the contracting offices and the number of contracts included in our review.

To assess patterns in DOD's, State's, and USAID's use of the unusual and compelling urgency exception to competition, we analyzed data from the Federal Procurement Data System-Next Generation (FPDS-NG). We included contracts and task orders coded as using the urgency exception under the field "reason not competed" from fiscal years 2010 through 2012 which represented the time period after the requirement to limit the duration of urgent contracts went into effect and reflected the most current reliable data to show trends over time. We determined that a contract was miscoded if it was coded in FPDS-NG as being awarded under the urgency exception, but our analysis of the contract file documentation showed that the contract was awarded using other procedures—such as the streamlined procedures under the simplified acquisition threshold—generally $150,000—or other exceptions to full and open competition such as national security. We analyzed DOD, State, and USAID obligation data and the types of goods and services based on product code fields. We assessed the reliability of FPDS-NG data by (1) performing electronic testing of required data elements, (2) reviewing existing information about the data and the system that produced them; and (3) comparing reported data to information from contract files that we sampled. In our analysis we excluded awards that were below $150,000 because of the high likelihood that these procurements followed simplified acquisition procedures which are separate from the procedures that apply to the urgency exception. Taking this approach allowed us to account for known data limitations. Thus, we determined that the federal procurement data were sufficiently reliable to examine patterns in DOD's, State's, and USAID's use of the urgency exception. To compare use of the urgency exception versus other exceptions to full and open competition, we conducted an analysis of the other values listed under the "reason not competed" field. In addition, we reviewed FPDS-NG instructions to identify protocols for entering contract data in the database and interviewed DOD, State, and USAID contracting officials and FPDS-NG subject matter experts about their procedures and processes for entering data in the procurement database.

To assess the reason that agencies awarded noncompetitive contracts on the basis of urgency and the extent to which justifications met FAR requirements, we performed an in depth review of contract files for 34 selected contracts that we determined—based on our review of contract file documentation and interviews with contracting officials—were awarded using the unusual and compelling urgency exception. Of the 62 contracts that we initially selected for our sample, we narrowed our analysis to 34 because 28 of the contracts were miscoded in FPDS-NG. For these 34 contracts, we reviewed contract file documentation such as acquisition plans, justifications and other documents agencies used to seek approval to limit competition on the selected contracts to determine agencies' rationale for using the urgency exception. We also reviewed DOD, State, and USAID guidance regarding the preparation and approval of justifications to use the urgency exception. Additionally, we reviewed the Federal Acquisition Regulation and reviewed agency policies and guidance to inform our analysis of the extent to which justifications met FAR requirements such as ensuring the justifications were signed by the appropriate individuals and made publicly available within the required timeframes. We compared agencies' policies and procedures with the *Standards for Internal Control in the Federal Government* which calls for documentation of transactions that is readily available for inspection, thus providing evidence of implementation.[1] We interviewed contracting and acquisition policy officials, procurement attorneys, program officials, and competition advocates at DOD, State, and USAID to discuss the facts and circumstances regarding use of the urgency exception and agency policies and procedures to implement FAR requirements for publicly posting justifications.

To determine the extent to which agencies complied with the FAR requirement to limit the total period of performance of a contract awarded using the urgency exception to no more than a year unless the head of the agency makes a determination of exceptional circumstances, we reviewed contract file documents for 34 selected contracts that we identified were awarded using the urgency exception. We also conducted legal research and interviewed contracting and acquisition policy officials at DOD, State, and USAID on the implementation of the duration requirement. We reviewed contract file documentation such as contract awards to determine the estimated period of performance. Further, we reviewed contract modifications and additional justifications prepared after award to determine the actual period of performance and action taken by the agencies when extending the period of performance for urgency contracts, such as preparing additional justifications for other than full and open or exercising the option to extend services. We also interviewed officials from the Office of Federal Procurement Policy within OMB to obtain their perspectives on the approaches that DOD, State, and USAID used to address the FAR requirement to limit the period of performance or obtain a determination from the head of the agency that exceptional circumstances necessitate a period of performance greater than 1 year. We also analyzed contract documents to identify instances where DOD, State, and USAID increased funding for the 34 contracts in our sample. We assessed the implications of inconsistent implementation of the FAR requirement to limit the period of performance of urgent contracts and the absence of an oversight mechanism to monitor increases in contract value against criteria in *Standards for Internal Control in the Federal Government*.[2] These criteria call for organizations to maintain proper controls that ensure transparency and accountability for stewardship of resources. To determine the extent to which DOD, State and USAID achieved competition with the use of the urgency exception, we interviewed contracting officials and reviewed contract documents, such as acquisition plans and price negotiation memorandums, to identify the barriers to competition that agencies cited and, to assess the extent to which the agencies solicited offers from multiple vendors.

We conducted this performance audit from March 2013 through March 2014 in accordance with generally accepted government auditing standards. Those standards require that we plan and perform the audit to obtain sufficient, appropriate evidence to provide a reasonable basis for our findings and conclusions based on our audit objectives. We believe that the evidence obtained provides a reasonable basis for our findings and conclusions based on our audit objectives.

APPENDIX II: SUMMARY OF CONTRACTS INCLUDED IN OUR SAMPLE

Of the 62 contracts included in our sample, we determined that 34 were awarded using the unusual and compelling urgency exception to competition.

Table 3 below provides an overview of the contracts in our sample including the awarding agency, a description of the item procured and the total dollars obligated. In addition, the table highlights the circumstances that, according to the Departments of Defense (DOD) and State, and the US Agency for International Development (USAID), led to use of the urgency exception such as to avoid a gap in program support or meet an urgent operational need.

Table 3. Summary of Contracts in Our Sample Awarded Under the Unusual and Compelling Urgency Exception

Item Procured	Funds obligated (in millions)	Contract Awarded to Meet an Urgent Operational Need	Contract Awarded to Avoid a gap in programming	Contract Awarded to meet other urgent needs[a]	Support missions in Afghanistan or Iraq
USAID					
Parliamentary support to the Afghanistan National Assembly	$4.9		●		Afghanistan
Financial audit services	$0.2			●	Afghanistan
Financial audit services	$0.2			●	Afghanistan
State					
Guard protection services	$178.1		●		Afghanistan
Ballistic resistant doors and window	$0.5			●	
Radio and television security equipment	$9.9			●	Afghanistan
Telecommuni cations and information technology services	$0.2			●	

Item Procured	**Funds obligated (in millions)**	**Contract Awarded to Meet an Urgent Operational Need**	**Contract Awarded to Avoid a gap in programming**	**Contract Awarded to meet other urgent needs[a]**	**Support missions in Afghanistan or Iraq**
Operations and maintenance support services at the U.S. Embassy compound in Baghdad, Iraq	$49.4		●		Iraq
Air Force					
Intelligence, surveillance and reconnaissance (ISR) airship	$114.9	●			Afghanistan
ISR unmanned aerial system	$14.9	●			Afghanistan
Secure communications equipment for ISR airship	$0.5	●			Afghanistan
Airborne system to protect against improvised explosive devices (IED)	$39.8	●			Afghanistan, Iraq
Professional support	$1.7		●		
Engineering support	$3.9		●		
Army					
Airborne radar equipment	$338.6	●			Afghanistan
Information technology and telecommunications services	$14.7		●		Afghanistan, Iraq

Table 3. (Continued)

Item Procured	Funds obligated (in millions)	Contract Awarded to Meet an Urgent Operational Need	Contract Awarded to Avoid a gap in programming	Contract Awarded to meet other urgent needs[a]	Support missions in Afghanistan or Iraq
Spare parts for the Persistent Threat Detection System.	$47.0	●			Afghanistan
Armored security vehicles	$525.4	●			Afghanistan
Equipment and accessories for tactical wheeled vehicles	$16.0			●	
Rocket propelled grenade net kits for tactical wheeled vehicles	$59.4	●			Afghanistan
Production of tactical wheeled vehicles	$177.6	●			Afghanistan
Management Support	$104.4		●		Afghanistan, Iraq
Personal armor	$4.4	●	●		Afghanistan
Navy					
Vehicle-mounted counter-IED system	$12.0	●			Afghanistan, Iraq
Mine identification and neutralization device	$48.2	●			

Item Procured	Funds obligated (in millions)	Contract Awarded to Meet an Urgent Operational Need	Contract Awarded to Avoid a gap in programming	Contract Awarded to meet other urgent needs[a]	Support missions in Afghanistan or Iraq
Ground Fault Interrupter for sonar system	$1.0			●	
Operational support for the Persistent Ground Surveillance System (PGSS)	$105.8	●			Afghanistan
PGSS spare parts and logistics support	$26.4	●	●		Afghanistan
Program support for PGSS operators	$6.4	●	●		Afghanistan
PGSS program support	$44.6	●	●		Afghanistan
Defense Logistics Agency					
Fuel	$31.8			●	
Jet fuel	$69.7		●		
Vehicle accessories for tactical wheeled vehicles	$4.7			●	Afghanistan, Iraq
Automatic fire extinguishing systems for tactical wheeled vehicles	$6.3			●	Afghanistan

Source: GAO analysis of contract documents.

[a] Other urgent needs include non-recurring urgent needs such as, construction of temporary work spaces, an unexpected break in oil refinery production, or support for a one time military mission.

APPENDIX III: DOD, STATE, AND USAID CONTRACTS THAT EXCEEDED 1 YEAR

Figure 7 highlights the items procured and the estimated versus actual duration of the 10 contracts we found with a period of performance of more than 1 year.

Agency	Contract	Contract duration
State	Guard protection services	12 18
USAID	Education and training services	7 16
Air Force	Intelligence, surveillance and reconnaissance airship	10 20
Air Force	Intelligence, surveillance and reconnaissance unmanned aerial system	13 26
Army	Program support	10 18
Army	Tactical wheeled vehicle upgrade kits	10 21
Army	Tactical wheeled vehicle modification	5 16
Army	Armored vehicles	12 40
Navy	Mine detection system	12 22
Navy	Vehicle mounted counter-improvised explosive device kits	7 17 [a]

Estimate in months

Actual in months

Source: GAO analysis of DOD contract documents.

[a]This undefinitized contract action had an estimated period of performance of 17 months at award. When definitized, the contract duration was shortened to 7 months.

Figure 7. Period of Performance for Contracts that Exceeded 1 Year.

End Notes

[1] Contracts awarded on the basis of an unusual and compelling urgency where the government may limit the number of sources from which it solicits bids or proposals are considered noncompetitive contracts. For the purposes of this report we refer to the unusual and compelling urgency exception to full and open competition as the urgency exception. We use the term limited competition to refer to situations when the government seeks offers from as many potential sources as is practical under the circumstances when using the urgency exception.

[2] 74 Fed. Reg. 52,849 (Oct. 14, 2009). In 2008, the Duncan Hunter National Defense Authorization Act for Fiscal Year 2009, Pub. L. No. 110-417, § 862, amended certain laws to require that contracts awarded using the urgency exception not exceed the time necessary to meet the unusual and compelling requirements and for the agency to enter into another contract, and may not exceed 1 year unless the head of the agency determines exceptional circumstances apply. The 2009 FAR amendment implemented this requirement.

[3] H.R. Rep. No. 112-705, at 817 (2012) (Conf. Rep.).

[4] GAO, Standards for Internal Control in the Federal Government, GAO/AIMD 00 21.3.1 (Washington, D.C.: November 1999).

[5] GAO/AIMD-00-21.3.1.

[6] Pub. L. No. 98-369, §§ 2711(a)(1) and 2723(a)(1), *codified as amended* at 41 U.S.C. § 3304 and 10 U.S.C. § 2304.

[7] In all, there are seven exceptions to full and open competition. See FAR § 6.302.

[8] Justifications are also to be posted to the procuring agency's website which may link to FedBizOpps. For most of the other exceptions to competition, justifications are to be published within 14 days of contract award.

[9] For example, urgency, exclusive licensing agreements, brand name or industrial mobilization. FAR 13.106-1(b)(1)(i).

[10] In our analysis we excluded awards that were below $150,000 because of the high likelihood that these procurements followed simplified acquisition procedures, which are separate from the procedures that apply to the urgency exception.

[11] Two of the contracts provided guard services to protect the U.S. embassies in Iraq and Afghanistan, while the third provided administrative support services to the National Visa Center.

[12] U.S. Agency for International Development Acquisition Regulation, § 706.302-70.

[13] We have previously reported on data reliability issues with FPDS-NG. See, e.g., GAO, *Federal Contracting: Observations on the Government's Contracting Data Systems,* GAO-09-1032T (Washington, D.C.: Sept. 29, 2009); *Improvements Needed to the Federal Procurement Data System-Next Generation,* GAO-05-960R (Washington, D.C.: Sept. 27, 2005).

[14] Going forward in this report, our analysis does not include the 28 contracts that were miscoded.

[15] Interim DOD Instruction 5000.02, "Operation of the Defense Acquisition System" (Nov. 25, 2013) and DOD "Acquisition Actions in Support of Joint Urgent Operational Needs" (Mar. 29, 2010).

[16] GAO, *Urgent Warfighter Needs: Opportunities Exist to Expedite Development and Fielding of Joint Capabilities*, GAO-12-385 (Washington, D.C.: Apr. 24, 2012).

[17] GAO, Defense Acquisitions*: Future Aerostat and Airship Investment Decisions Drive Oversight and Coordination Needs,* GAO-13-81 (Washington, D.C.: Oct. 23, 2012). DOD,

Office of the Inspector General, Air Force and Army Corps of Engineers Improperly Managed the Award of Contracts for the Blue Devil Block 2 Persistent Surveillance System (Sept. 19, 2013).

[18] GAO-13-81.

[19] GAO-12-385.

[20] In general, justifications for the other exceptions to full and open competition must be posted within 14 days of award.

[21] GAO/AIMD-00-21.3.1.

[22] The Army has draft guidance which is in the final stages of review.

[23] The contractor completed the work in less than 1 year; however, a determination from the head of the agency would still have been required at the time of contract award because the undefinitized contract appears to have had a period of performance of more than 1 year.

[24] These extensions of contract performance are not exclusive to urgency contracts.

[25] FAR 52.217-8 "Option to Extend Services" is included in solicitations and contracts for services when the inclusion of an option is appropriate.

[26] Modifications that are outside the original scope of the contract—such as changes to requirements, quantities and period performance—must comply with competition requirements—and agencies must prepare justifications for other than full and open competition. See, e.g., Neal R. Gross & Co., Inc., B-237434, Feb. 23, 1990, 90-1 CPD ¶ 212 at 2-3.

[27] GAO has previously reported on the risks associated with undefinitized contract actions, which authorize DOD contractors to begin work before reaching a final agreement on contract terms and must be definitized within certain parameters described in DOD regulation. See GAO, *Defense Contracting: DOD Has Enhanced Insight into Undefinitized Contract Action Use, but Management at Local Commands Needs Improvement*, GAO-10-299 (Washington, D.C.: Jan. 28, 2010).

[28] GAO/AIMD-00-21.3.1.

[29] GAO, *Defense Acquisitions: DOD Efforts to Adopt Open Systems for Its Unmanned Aircraft Systems Have Progressed Slowly,* GAO-13-651, (Washington D.C.: July 31, 2013)

[30] GAO, *Defense Management: Opportunities to Enhance the Implementation of Performance-Based Logistics,* GAO-04-715 (Washington, D.C.: Aug. 16, 2004); *Weapons Acquisition: DOD Should Strengthen Policies for Assessing Technical Data Needs to Support Weapons Systems,* GAO-06-839 (Washington, D.C.: July 14, 2006); and *Defense Acquisition: DOD Should Clarify Requirements for Assessing and Documenting Technical-Data Needs*, GAO-11-469 (Washington, D.C.: May 11, 2011).

[31] The PTDS program has competitively awarded three contracts to procure operators for the aerostat since 2006. These three contracts were awarded to the same contractor.

[32] GAO, *Defense Contracting*: *Actions Needed to Increase Competition*, GAO-13-325 (Washington, D.C.: March 28, 2013).

End Notes for Appendix I

[1] GAO/AIMD-00-21.3.1.

[2] GAO/AIMD-00-21.3.1.

INDEX

A

B

C

D

M

N

O

P

Q

R

S

T

V

W